A Castle in the Wilderness

THE STORY OF THE BANFF SPRINGS HOTEL

"Banff Springs Hotel. Finely situated on a bluff above the confluence of the Bow and the Spray. 1½ miles from the railway station, with hot sulphur baths open air swimming, tennis court, and bowling alley. Good cuisine and attendance. $3½ – 4."

– Baedeker's Canada, 1894

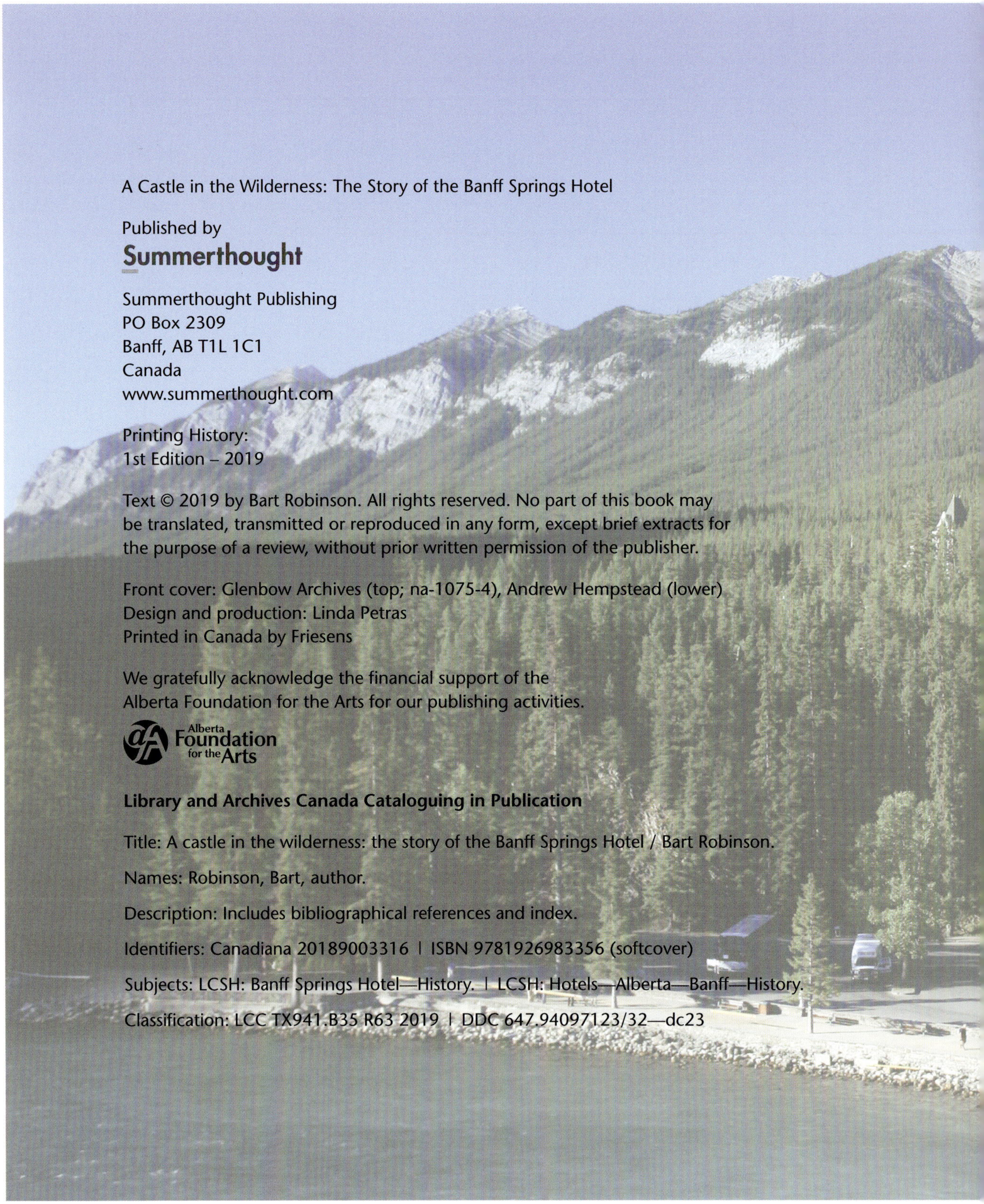

A Castle in the Wilderness: The Story of the Banff Springs Hotel

Published by
Summerthought

Summerthought Publishing
PO Box 2309
Banff, AB T1L 1C1
Canada
www.summerthought.com

Printing History:
1st Edition – 2019

Front cover: Glenbow Archives (top; na-1075-4), Andrew Hempstead (lower)
Design and production: Linda Petras
Printed in Canada by Friesens

We gratefully acknowledge the financial support of the Alberta Foundation for the Arts for our publishing activities.

Alberta Foundation for the Arts

Library and Archives Canada Cataloguing in Publication

Title: A castle in the wilderness: the story of the Banff Springs Hotel / Bart Robinson.

Names: Robinson, Bart, author.

Description: Includes bibliographical references and index.

Identifiers: Canadiana 20189003316 | ISBN 9781926983356 (softcover)

Subjects: LCSH: Banff Springs Hotel—History. | LCSH: Hotels—Alberta—Banff—History.

Classification: LCC TX941.B35 R63 2019 | DDC 647.94097123/32—dc23

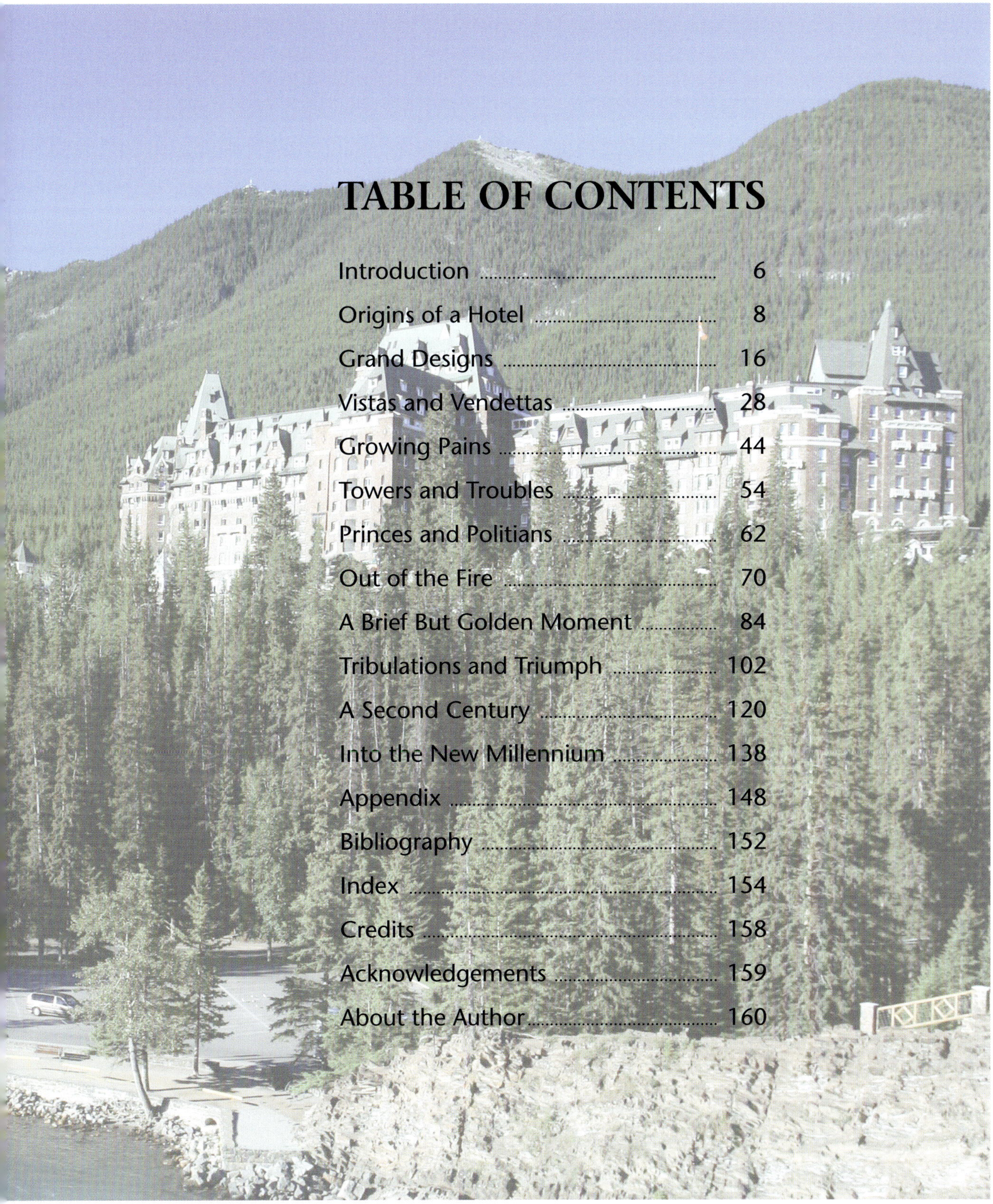

TABLE OF CONTENTS

Introduction 6
Origins of a Hotel 8
Grand Designs 16
Vistas and Vendettas 28
Growing Pains 44
Towers and Troubles 54
Princes and Politians 62
Out of the Fire 70
A Brief But Golden Moment 84
Tribulations and Triumph 102
A Second Century 120
Into the New Millennium 138
Appendix 148
Bibliography 152
Index 154
Credits 158
Acknowledgements 159
About the Author 160

The original Banff Springs Hotel viewed from the top of Tunnel Mountain.

Introduction

"IT HAD NO BUSINESS BEING THERE."

When Morley Roberts, an aging English author, world-traveller, and one-time railway navvy, rolled into Banff in the summer of 1925 it had been 41 years since he'd first visited the area. Things had changed. Expected, perhaps, was that Old Man Goss, who once ran the moonshine still on Whiskey Creek, had long since disappeared, perhaps a victim of his own libations. More surprising was that the town itself was no longer Siding 29, a dusty scattering of shacks and tents at the foot of Cascade Mountain, but Banff, a bustling alpine village straddling the Bow River and boldly claiming to be the centre of the greatest mountain playground on the continent. Of all the changes Roberts witnessed, however, nothing compared to the shocking sight of a castle rising from the valley floor on the far side of the river. The idea of a rock palace in the wilderness was too much to fathom: "It had no business being there," he said, "for when I was thereabouts so long ago no one could have thought of it."

Roberts toured the castle—touched its walls, peered through its windows, talked to its inhabitants—and decided that, like Banff itself, it was a dream, at once beautiful and absurd. It wasn't a dream, of course, but it was decidedly beautiful. And if its presence in the wilderness was absurd, well, there was a method to its madness.

Today, nearly a century after Roberts' return to the Bow Valley, the Banff Springs Hotel continues to prompt the same incredulity the old man felt in 1925. The castle's dreamlike qualities have endured, and first-time visitors' questions are nearly programmed in their similarity: "What's *that*? What's it doing here? Who built it? Who owns it? Why? When? What for?" To answer those questions, one must go back to the years following Canada's confederation and read the news about a struggling young company called the Canadian Pacific Railway.

Railway crew on hand car, 1888.

Banff Avenue, 1887.

Origins of a Hotel

"SINCE WE CAN'T EXPORT THE SCENERY, WE'LL HAVE TO IMPORT THE TOURISTS."

The Canadian Pacific Railway (CPR) was never, by any normal standard, a modest child. Born the wealthy scion of economic necessity and political intrigue—two well-acquainted if not exactly well-respected bedfellows—its mere conception toppled John A. Macdonald's first government in 1873. Five years later, when Macdonald was again in power and the idea was reintroduced, it became cause for some of the greatest uproars ever known in an institution noted for great uproars. Words such as "liar" and "coward" were bandied freely in the parliamentary chambers. Liberal doomsayers foresaw the day when the young company would become the proprietor of the Canadian government. But the Canadian Railway Bill, guaranteeing the company government support of 25 million dollars, 25 million acres of land, a 20-year monopoly of Western trade, and freedom from taxes on all holdings in perpetuity, was passed by the Senate and became law February 15, 1881.

"Like the Roman roadbuilders in primitive Europe, the Canadian railway builders in primitive North America knew that they could best profit from the wilderness, and protect their interests as well, by bringing a little civilization to its barbarian heart."

– Abraham Rogatnick, 1968

The CPR had no reason to be a modest child, for railway building in Canada, as in Bismarck's Germany, Grant's America, and Cavour's Italy, was synonymous with nation building. The support the CPR received was an accurate reflection of the young country's impatience to fulfill its Victorian pioneering ambitions, as measured by the replacement of wilderness by civilization. No one could deny a transcontinental railway would help tame the interior.

Politically, the railway was expected to tie up "the rags and ends of Confederation," joining British Columbia with the Eastern provinces. Economically, it would give the tiring St. Lawrence commercial empire some fresh blood and prise open the Canadian interior's vast marketing possibilities. The CPR, in fact, promised its country even more. In an 1889 publication, *The New Highway to the Orient*, the company referred to itself as a young giant whose "arms at once reached out across that broad ocean and grasped the teas and silks of China and Japan to exchange for the fabrics of Europe and North America."

To make good its claim, the company needed more than a flow of grand words along the new tracks, and it was soon involved in constructing new facilities to feed and support the trains and their cargoes as they moved along the national artery. The dining pavilion was one such support. It arose from an obvious need for passengers to retire for relaxation and refreshment from time to time during what could be a physically demanding and often tedious journey. From

BANFF'S FIRST VISITORS

While archaeologists once believed the mountains and the challenging environment of the Bow Valley severely limited their use by prehistoric Indigenous communities, a Banff National Park survey in 1969–1970 turned up a surprising 125 sites. One of them, near Lake Minnewanka, yielded a Clovis point that suggested humans might have been in the valley as early as 12,000 years ago.

The rethinking of the valley's human occupation was further fuelled in 1983 when a more in-depth survey was undertaken as part of the requirements for the twinning of the Trans-Canada Highway. That survey, too, unearthed multiple sites, the best known of which was discovered on the north shore of what was once a much larger Vermilion Lake. As Banff historian Ted Hart has written, the discovery was "a very rich site showing evidence of seven separate living levels and multiple occupations by different peoples, each sequentially covered up when mud and loose rock from the slopes of Mounts Norquay and Cory slid down over them."

The site confirmed that the valley had been used for seasonal hunting and gathering for close to 11,000 years, beginning with nomadic bison-hunting peoples from the prairies. Other sites, dating to more recent times, led archaeologists to surmise that the valley and other parts of the park were also occupied, seasonally but recurrently, by fish-eating peoples from the interior of British Columbia. In 1998, Parks Canada archaeologist Gwynn Langemann, understanding that the valley near Banff had been not only occupied for a very long time but was also the meeting place of peoples from both east and west, concluded that Banff "was already a village" well before the first Europeans entered the mountains.

In more recent centuries, a variety of Indigenous peoples visited the valley, not only to hunt and gather but also to make use of Sulphur Mountain's hot springs. They included the Ktunaxa (Kootenay), the Piikani (Peigan), the Cree, and the Shoshone (Snake), who converged on the valley from, respectively, the west, the east, the north, and the south. Later, in the mid-1700s, a new group, the Nakoda (Stoney) of the Sioux Nation, penetrated the mountains via the North Saskatchewan, Bow, and Highwood Rivers to become frequent visitors of what is now Banff National Park. Their deep relationship with the region is summed up by the title of Nakoda chief John Snow's book *These Mountains are our Sacred Places* (1977).

The earliest known rendering of the Banff townsite, painted in 1888 by the station agent, D. Clark.

this elemental necessity, the CPR's grandiose hotels arose.

Such resting spots could have been simple structures—even shunted railway cars—and still fulfilled their purpose. That they were not, and that they became instead internationally famous hotels equated with royalty and representing the apex of elegant living, is due to the indefatigable energies of William Cornelius Van Horne, the man who "capitalized the scenery" of the Canadian West.

Tourism, Van Horne believed, was one way of getting people to use his railway, and he was fully aware of the dollar potential in the Canadian Rockies. Always a man to plunge to the heart of things, he summed up his philosophy succinctly: "Since we can't export the scenery, we'll have to import the tourists." Accordingly, with characteristic energy and dispatch, he launched a campaign to entice the crème de la crème of the international set to the wilds of Western Canada.

One of the cornerstones of the plan—and the realization of one of Van Horne's most cherished dreams—was the establishment of a system of luxurious hotels commanding the most scenic views of the Canadian Rockies. An avid amateur architect, Van Horne took great pleasure in sketching, modifying, and remodifying the designs for such structures. His goal was a series of lodgings that would offer royal-calibre guests all the comforts of home but still afford them the exhilaration of wilderness contact. Who could resist? The promotion for the campaign painted a tantalizing picture:

May I not tempt you, kind reader, to leave England for a few short weeks and journey with me across that broad land, the beauties and glories of which have so recently been brought to within our reach? There will be no hardships to endure, no difficulties to overcome, and no dangers or annoyances whatever. You shall see mighty rivers, vast forests, boundless plains, stupendous mountains and wonders innumerable; and you shall see all in comfort, nay, in luxury.

With such luxurious accommodation in mind, the company began constructing three "Railway Dining Stations" in 1886, less than a year after the driving of the last spike of the transcontinental railway at Craigellachie, British Columbia. Mount Stephen House at Field, Fraser Canyon Hotel at North Bend, and Glacier House at Rogers Pass, all in British Columbia and all modelled after Swiss chalets, rapidly became popular alpine resorts. Glacier House in particular, at the heart of North America's "Little Switzerland," did such a booming business that the CPR hired Swiss mountain guides to guide climbs in the Rogers Pass area. While architect

WILLIAM VAN HORNE: THE ABLEST RAILROAD GENERAL IN THE WORLD

"I drink all I can, I eat all I can, and I don't give a damn for anyone."

Born in Illinois in 1843, William Cornelius Van Horne began working on railroads at age 14. He was an apt and energetic employee, and a quick study when it came to learning all aspects of the industry—including driving a locomotive. He was named general superintendent of the Chicago, Milwaukee, St. Paul and Pacific Railroad at age 35 and, just

William Van Horne (centre, with hands in pockets) and CPR officials at Stoney Creek in 1894.

Thomas Charles Roby is credited with the design of the first three chalets, it is likely that Van Horne played an important part in developing their common look: a three-storey centre section with two wings of different heights extending in opposite directions.

But these modest structures were merely appetizers for a man like Van Horne. Even as the first three hotels were being built, he was scheming about constructing another, larger, grander hotel in the heart of the Canadian Rockies.

Deciding to build a substantial, luxurious hotel in the Bow Valley in the mid-1880s required considerable audacity. Although Siding 29 had received a boost in stature in 1884 by being renamed for Banffshire County in Scotland—the birthplace of then CPR president George Stephen—it was not yet the sort of place a young person in search of

four years later, in 1882, was recruited to be the general manager of the Canadian Pacific Railway. Tasked to oversee the construction of the nation's first transcontinental railway, he had within two years become vice president of the line and earned a reputation as the "ablest railroad general in the world." In 1888, he succeeded George Stephen as CPR president.

Part robber baron, part Renaissance man, and always a larger-than-life character with an all-consuming passion for life, Van Horne was equally at home playing an all-night round of poker with the railway navvies or traversing the stormy politics of nation building with powerful politicians and wealthy CPR investors. He repeatedly travelled from one end of Canada to the other, watching over his newborn railway like an anxious prairie hen watching over her brood. A firm believer that if the company wasn't moving full speed ahead it was moving backward, he gave no quarter in pushing the project forward, a determination that saw the railway finished in less than half the projected time.

To Van Horne, a railway was much more than tracks and cars. A communications system, he believed, should be an integral part of the transportation system, and the transportation system should extend beyond the end of the line. In 1891, in pursuit of the latter objective, he created a sea transport division for the CPR that carried passengers and cargo between Vancouver and Hong Kong. And, as evidenced in his promotion of the CPR hotels, he believed in fine passenger accommodation both on and off the tracks.

Although best known for his railroad work, Van Horne was a person of multiple interests and talents. Among other things, he was a painter, an art collector (with a special interest in Japanese porcelain and French Impressionist paintings), a sculptor, a violinist, an architect, a fossil collector, a botanist, and a gardener.

Once he moved to Canada, he stayed, living with his wife and children in what became known as the Van Horne Mansion in Montreal's Golden Square Mile. He died in September 1915 having accomplished in 72 years what would take most mortals several lifetimes.

His influence has been long lasting: in 2000, more than eight decades after his death, he was selected from a field of 118 individuals in Canada's Business Hall of Fame as the most outstanding business leader of the past 100 years.

Dating to September 1886, this is one of the oldest known photos of the Banff townsite. It was taken from the top of Tunnel Mountain.

cosmopolitan fame and fortune would choose to settle. Situated in a meadow at the foot of Cascade Mountain about three kilometres (two miles) north of the present town, its amassed potential lay in a boxcar railway station, a few ramshackle buildings, two small hotels, three stores, and a livery stable.

However, as Van Horne and his influential acquaintances from Eastern Canada had determined, the sleepy little collection of rough-hewn buildings and muddy streets held promise. In the combination of a stunning mountain backdrop and nearby medicinal mineral hot springs lay a seed that, properly tended, would blossom into one of the world's most famous mountain playgrounds.

Not surprisingly, Van Horne proved to be an adept gardener. Even as the railway's route through the Canadian Rockies was being scouted, Van Horne and his CPR colleagues were witnessing the mutually beneficial relationship that had evolved in the US between the Northern Pacific Railroad and Yellowstone National Park following the park's establishment in 1872. As noted by CPR chief engineer Sandford Fleming, a series of mountain parks made accessible by the railway would draw "sportsmen and crowds of tourists . . . to enjoy the pure air and the charm of the scenery and the striking features of beauty nowhere else to be seen."

Van Horne, understanding the profitable symbiosis that could be coaxed from a mixture of fine accommodation, spectacular scenery, and mountain recreation, endorsed the creation of a 26-square-kilometre (10-square-mile) "Hot Springs Reservation." Officially designated by Order in Council 2197 in 1885, the new reserve was intended to secure their control for the Crown.

In the last quarter of the 19th century, creating national parks was as fitting an instrument for building nations as creating railways, and in June 1887, the Hot Springs Reservation became the core of Rocky Mountains Park of Canada. Encompassing 670 square kilometres (260 square miles) of jaw-dropping mountain landscape, the new park was "reserved and set apart as a public park and pleasure ground for the benefit, advantage and enjoyment of the people of Canada." While "Banff" was suggested as a name for the park in 1887, it wasn't until 1930 and the passage of the National Parks Act that Rocky Mountains Park officially became Banff National Park.

The changes in the Bow Valley's land tenure were reflected by changes in Banff itself. The hot springs were attracting increasing attention and their promoters were comparing them to the great thermal waters at Bath (England) and Baden-Baden (Germany). In the summer of 1886, cows could still stroll down the town's main street, but there was a decided entrepreneurial air about the place. New buildings for new business were going up, and a new carriage road and a floating bridge across the Bow River were being built to transport eager bathers from the railway station to the hot springs. The biggest change, however, came late that fall, when it was announced that Banff itself would follow the new road south to a new site closer to the Bow River and the hot springs. According to one source, the move was inspired at least in part by the coming construction of the Banff Springs Hotel.

BANFF: AN 1880s TOWNSITE TIMELINE

1881: A meadow at the foot of Cascade Mountain became known as Aylmer Park, the first European name for the Banff area. The namesake, Fred Aylmer, was a noted CPR surveyor from Quebec who helped run the preliminary railway line into the valley and then used a period of unanticipated unemployment to explore its environs.

One of the first buildings at Siding 29 was this log shack built by CPR workers Ben and Fred Woodworth in 1884.

1883: A railway siding is a short section of track separate from the main line that is used to store extra cars or allow two trains to pass each other when they are running on the main track in opposite directions. On October 27, 1883, such a siding was laid near Aylmer Park. Following the CPR's numeric-based system of naming sidings, it was called Siding 29.

1884: A boxcar station was constructed at Siding 29, which was beginning to show some commercial potential based on its proximity to the Sulphur Mountain hot springs. In turn, Siding 29 was renamed Banff by Lord Strathcona (Donald Alexander Smith), a CPR cofounder and director. "Banff" was chosen in recognition of Banffshire County in Scotland, the birthplace of CPR president George Stephen.

1886: A new location for Banff was selected and surveyed. The new site, on the banks of the Bow River, was closer to the Cave and Basin and Upper Hot Springs than the previous location and better situated to accommodate a "business town." One source suggests the site was selected, at least in part, in anticipation of the Banff Springs Hotel's being built on the far side of the river.

The original Banff Springs Hotel in winter.

Grand Designs

"A FEW FACTS ABOUT THE MAMMOUTH [SIC] BUILDING AS BEING ERECTED AT BANFF."

Credit for the Banff Springs Hotel's picturesque location generally goes to Tom Wilson, a young CPR guide and packer who had been working in the Bow Valley for two or three years before the railway arrived. When he heard Van Horne was planning to build his hotel at the foot of Tunnel Mountain on the Bow River's north bank, Wilson approached the railroad general and said he could show him a better site. After crossing the river, the two men walked to a forested promontory that not only overlooked the rushing cataract of the Bow Falls but was also within a rock's throw of the Bow's confluence with the Spray River. Even better, it commanded a sweeping view down the Bow Valley to the Fairholme Range, framed perfectly by the limestone cliffs of Tunnel Mountain and Mount Rundle. Van Horne agreed: it was a site worthy of his grand ambition.

To design a building that was the equal of its location, Van Horne hired Bruce Price, the architectural high priest of the Boston baronage. Price was already known for the parlour cars with bay windows he had designed for the Pennsylvania Railroad and the Boston and Albany Railroad, and he had been commissioned to design the CPR's Windsor Station in Montreal. Shortly thereafter, in 1886, Van Horne asked him to submit plans for the hotel at Banff.

Bruce Price, architect of the first Banff Springs Hotel.

In a flurry of correspondence between the two men, Price outlined his ideas for the new hotel.

I send herewith a sketch and plans of the proposed Hotel at Banff . . . There are 92 master rooms and 18 steward rooms. The kitchen wing is intended to be a frame and sheathed one story structure built in the economical manner. The heating and its plant and fuel bins could be placed under the Dining Room.

Price sired two noteworthy and enduring social entities. One was daughter Emily Post, the apostle of American etiquette; the other was Canada's "national style" of architecture, in the form of the medieval French château. While it takes an active imagination to draw a link between the daughter and the national style, one Price critic was able to do so by suggesting Emily's "rationalization of anachronistic social behaviour mirrored her father's ability to do the same for architecture." Such opinions aside, and despite his irregular reputation, Price is without question one of the important individuals in the history of Canadian architecture.

At the time of Price's CPR commissions, Canadian builders were slowly edging towards agreement on an appropriate architectural style for the young nation, with the debate strongly influenced by the British High Victorian Gothic's revival. The essence of Victorian architecture was that public structures should have both architectural "reality" and "meaning," and Great Britain had settled upon the Gothic style to deliver both. In Canada, the prevailing assumption was that the Dominion could do no better than follow suit. That it did so is well evidenced in the ribbed vaulting, pointed arches, and flying buttresses of the houses of Parliament in Ottawa and University College in Toronto, which are structures of the 1850s.

By the 1880s, however, two divergent trends emerged that would have great bearing on the future of North American architecture. One was "organicism," the idea that a building

AT THE CENTRE OF IT ALL: THE BANFF HOT SPRINGS

The "Springs" in "Banff Springs Hotel" was inserted to highlight the greatest attraction of the Bow Valley at the time of the hotel's building: Sulphur Mountain's hot mineral springs. Although Indigenous communities from east and west of the Rockies had been using the waters not only for bathing but also for medicinal and spiritual purposes for millennia, the springs came to national prominence with the CPR's arrival. Several early European explorers of the Bow Valley noted the hot springs' presence on both the north and south flanks of Sulphur Mountain, but credit for their "discovery" generally goes to three young railway workers: Frank McCabe and the brothers William and Thomas McCardell.

In August 1883, taking some time off from their railway work, the three men went prospecting on Sulphur Mountain and stumbled upon something that, while not gold, was potentially just as precious. The big strike was two adjacent hot springs—one occupying a circular pool on the mountainside and the other occupying a subterranean cavern accessible only via a perilous descent through a small hole in the cavern's roof.

Knowing how popular natural hot springs were around the world, the men reasoned that their discovery would soon be attracting a steady stream of wealthy international bathers and health seekers. Building a fence around the springs and constructing a crude cabin, McCabe and the McCardells began the long process of establishing a claim to the site of what would come to be known as the Cave and Basin.

Unfortunately for the three, the CPR and the Dominion government were by then also aware of the springs and their value. Van Horne, after being belayed by a stout rope into the cave, emerged to declare, "These springs are worth a million dollars!" Following a hearing into the validity of what had quickly become numerous claims of ownership, the government, acknowledging that the various Sulphur Mountain hot springs promised "to be of great sanitary advantage for the public," took control of the area and established the Banff Hot Springs Reservation in 1885. Bathhouses were installed in 1887 with bathers paying 10 cents for a swim.

Today, the only springs open for bathing are the Upper Hot Springs. The Cave and Basin pools are closed, but the Cave and Basin National Historic Site remains one of Banff's most popular attractions. Interpretive displays describe the springs' natural and human history, and a narrow tunnel winds into the dimly lit cave, where visitors can view the subterranean pool and look for Banff Springs snails, a rare and endangered species found nowhere in the world but the hot springs of Sulphur Mountain.

should be a natural, organic extension of the surrounding environment. The other was the Beaux-Arts movement, based on the notion that "reality" in architecture could best be expressed through precedents of the past made bigger and better with the technologies and materials of the present.

Although Price won his reputation as a master of the Beaux-Arts, he was well acquainted with organicism and no stranger to good old-fashioned architectural symbolism. In the 16th century Châteaux of the Loire—characterized by flat, crisp walls, steep roofs, a central tower, and round turrets flanking the doors—he found a structure he thought combined all three: the symbol, the architectural reality, and a style that organically befitted a northern climate and rugged landscape. As for improving on the

Bathers in the Basin, circa 1885.

Bruce Price's original sketch for the Banff Springs Hotel. The completed hotel differed from the sketch in that it lacked the pyramidal portion of the roof.

style of the past, Price was pleased to note that he "had the entire resources of the Canadian Pacific Railway to draw upon, and hence it was possible to build with certain materials in certain ways."

> *"Whatever is picturesque in a design should be accomplished by the exigencies of the site rather than deliberately made . . . A truly picturesque effect can never be produced deliberately . . . It can only be had by adding part to part and without deliberate design or intent."*
>
> – Bruce Price, 1899

While some architectural historians have stated that Price's creations were more archaeologically than organically oriented, and that they were built to convey the idea of luxury at the expense of the environment, his buildings nevertheless exhibited the important hallmarks of Late Victorian architecture. They were visually clean and attractive, pleasing in line and colour, well adapted to a picturesque site, and without exception capable of exciting all but the very dullest of imaginations. The style, in fact, proved so exciting, so "very right" for Canada, that it became the focal point of Canadian architecture. And Price, unwittingly, became the father of a style that remained vigorous until the 1940s. Indeed, the château style was so influential that throughout the early 1900s, it was the only architectural mode acceptable for government structures. Price's own Canadian works include Windsor Station (Montreal), Place Viger Hotel and Station (Montreal), Château Frontenac (Quebec City), and, of course, the original Banff Springs Hotel.

Although little information exists about construction of Price's original hotel, it is known that building commenced in the fall of 1886, the same year the plans were commissioned. As the number of local labourers at the time would not have exceeded

70, most of the building was done by railway workers, many of whom were Chinese and brought to Banff specifically for the job.

> *"There is a large class of buildings erected by Mr. Price in which the French architecture of the early part of the XVI century has been used with great freedom and intelligence."*
>
> – Russell Sturgis, 1899

The notion of a stylish, sophisticated hotel arising in the hinterlands—an endeavour involving noteworthy amounts of imagination, boldness, and capital—caught the attention of the Canadian press. An 1887 article in the *Winnipeg Sun*, entitled "The Great Hotel: A few Facts About the Mammouth [sic] Building as Being Erected at Banff," gave Manitobans the latest information on the project:

The hotel, which will be built by the company, the work being done under the supervision of their own officials, is to be a mammouth [sic] affair, and to contain 250 beds. It is to be constructed entirely of timber, three stories in height with a dormer in the roof, and a basement excavated in rock; it will be in two main wings, the front being the largest, and this will contain a rotunda, rising to the height of the building, and an elevator. The rear wing will be devoted mainly to the commissariat and domestic apartments. The hotel will have its own gas and water works, and also be supplied with electric lights and electric appliances.

In architectural fact, the building emerged a somewhat different creature from the one for which CPR general superintendent William

Construction of the Banff Springs Hotel began in 1886 and continued until 1888.

Whyte carried blueprints across the nation. No one remembers the name of the person in charge of construction, but it is well known and recorded that when Van Horne eased his ample girth into Banff in the summer of 1887, he found the rapidly rising hotel turned 180 degrees from what the plans called for. This had the disastrous effect of affording the kitchen staff the "million dollar view" of the confluence of the Bow and the Spray Rivers, and left the guests in their rotunda viewing the pine trees on the flanks of Sulphur Mountain.

Van Horne was not amused. As one of his colleagues stated, "Van Horne was one of the most considerate and even-tempered of men, but when an explosion came it was magnificent." Even in his most explosive moments, however, Van Horne could focus on whatever the issue was, and by the time the reverberations of his voice had echoed into the further reaches of the Bow Valley, he had sketched a new pavilion and ordered that it be built behind the kitchen, thus resurrecting the coveted view.

Van Horne's architectural acumen and legendary speed of response were illustrated again a bit later, when someone asked about plans for a new railway station in Banff. Van Horne reputedly snatched up a piece of brown paper, sketched in a few hurried lines, and handed it back to the inquirer: "Lots of good logs there. Cut them, peel them, and build your station."

Despite misread blueprints and other lesser catastrophes, work proceeded rapidly, and by the early spring of 1888, the building

Banff Railway Station in 1888, the year the Banff Springs Hotel opened.

One of the earliest photos of the Banff Springs Hotel, taken just after its opening in 1888.

was nearing completion. The structure, as early accounts and photographs portray it, was a frame building of three storeys and a dormered roof. From above, it resembled the letter *H*, with two wings—one to the east and one to the west—forming the vertical components of the letter. The new pavilion jutted out towards the river from the front (east) wing. The exterior was veneered to resemble cream-coloured Winnipeg brick and was trimmed with oil-finished cedar shingles from British Columbia. The building's romantic medieval air was accentuated by steep-hipped roofs with pointed dormers, corner turrets, and large bay windows.

Debates about the building's stylistic sources raged. One traveller referred to its being "in the Schloss style of the Rhenish provinces," while another believed it to be "something like a wooden combination of the Tudor hall and Swiss chalet." Yet another was correct in assuming that the French château was the hotel's inspiration, but then went on to surmise that it was built "as a gesture of recognition to the French-Canadian population and in tribute to the French explorers who had blazed the trail for the Canadian Pacific," a thought that, although plausible, probably never entered Price's head.

The interior was as visually stimulating as the exterior. Finished in native pine and fir, it was dominated by a huge glass-covered octagonal rotunda that served as the building's main lobby. The structure's upper floors opened

An 1888 illustration of the Banff Springs Hotel from the London Illustrated News.

The main lobby of the Banff Springs Hotel, photographed in the late 1880s.

onto the central hall in balconies in successive galleries, making it possible for the guests to leave their bedrooms "and gape down at the company assembled there." A large reading room, various parlours, dining rooms, smoking rooms, offices, and a few guest rooms occupied any ground-floor area not taken by the central rotunda, while most of the area in the upper two storeys was devoted to guest accommodation; many of the rooms were en suite.

Aside from housing the machinery for the electric lights, the basement sported a fine bar and billiard room for gentlemen guests seeking a retreat from mountain scenery and, in the order of the day, perhaps a dignified respite from their wives. A separate building housed boilers for steam heat and a large bathhouse. The bathhouse, with 10 separate bathing rooms and a common 9-by-24-metre plunge pool, was fed by hot mineral waters piped down from the lower slopes of Sulphur Mountain.

Such, then, was the state of the Banff Springs Hotel when it opened its doors on June 5, 1888, under the watchful eye of the first manager, George Holliday.

HOW MUCH DID IT COST?

Approximate price of goods when the Banff Springs Hotel opened in 1888:

A postcard	$0.02
A loaf of bread	$0.06
1 pound of steak	$0.12
1 pound of coffee	$0.19
A pair of shoes	$2
A night at the Banff Springs Hotel meals included	$3
A wagon	$85
A CPR round-trip ticket, Montreal to Vancouver	$85
A horse	$175
Banff Springs Hotel's total construction cost	$250,000

An early CPR postcard.

Looking down the Bow River from the hotel, 1890.

Vistas and Vendettas

"THE DINING ROOM IS NOT SO GOOD, BEING REMINISCENT OF AN ITALIAN CONVENT TURNED INTO A BARRACK."

While some of the early guests of the Banff Springs Hotel might have taken issue with Van Horne's proclamation that it was the "Finest Hotel on the North American Continent," few would argue about the superiority of its ambience. From the dining rooms with their exclusive French service to the plush comforts of the smoking and reading rooms, an air of rarefied extravagance permeated the building.

Van Horne and Price set out to create a specific type of atmosphere by constructing an edifice adorned with all the accoutrements of a romantic past. They succeeded splendidly in their task. "Did it matter," asks one historian, speaking of the early CPR château hotels in general, "if their size disguised a fundamental formlessness, their exotic detail was meaningless, their treatment of materials and plan monotonous and artificial?" Not at all, as long as the hotels hit their symbolic mark with an opulent presentation of historic elegance. If the guests couldn't quite put their collective finger on the Banff Springs Hotel's archaeological precedents, they could at least make their conjectures in sumptuous, well-attended surroundings.

The hotel's significance, however, extended well beyond the pleasure of its individual guests. Along with other CPR hotels—in Montreal, Quebec City, Vancouver, Lake Louise, Field, North Bend, and Rogers Pass—the Banff Springs played an important social role for the wealthy elites of Canadian society, helping fill the cultural vacuum found on the western side of the Atlantic. At the turn of the 20th century, capitalism, laissez-faire, and

An early 1890s CPR brochure cover advertising the company's hotels.

The original Banff Springs Hotel, viewed from Surprise Corner, features the Van Horne Pavilion jutting out from the east wing of the hotel. Surprise Corner, a rocky bluff overlooking the Bow River at Bow Falls, provides a viewpoint of the hotel that has been irresistible to photographers since the 1880s.

W.L. Mathews, manager of the Banff Springs Hotel, poses on horseback with staff and guests at the Bow Falls in the 1890s.

the lack of a federal income tax combined to create great personal fortunes both in Canada and the United States, and the young empire-builders were determined to prove themselves worthy of their newfound wealth. For them, the hotels presented a chance "to pose in the elegant costume of an age of social class, which suggested that those who entered the ballrooms of the place were invited guests of rank, gentlemen and ladies of importance, squires rather than peasants." And for the Europeans of established wealth, the hotels were a demonstration that Canada was not wanting for cultural habitation and propriety.

Whatever its social province, the Banff Springs was an impressive structure, "a stately pile," as one journalist put it, and it never failed to draw (frequently overwrought) praise from first-time visitors. Fortunately, the published travel journal, a Victorian institution, has preserved many of these accolades, and a random sampling establishes that the hotel was "comfortable and daring," "one of the finest structures of its kind in Canada," "a most sumptuous affair, as palatial as a Monterey or Saratoga hotel," "a wonder of art and invention in the wilderness," and finally, outdoing even Van Horne's edict, "the best mountain hotel in the world."

The guests who held such opinions were a varied lot, but all found common denominators in their wealth and their mode of transportation—the train. Staying at the hotel in its early years was rarely an end in itself but rather one of several stops on a long and arduous, albeit exciting, transcontinental

A four-horse tally-ho at the entrance of the original Banff Springs Hotel. The wagons were used to transport guests to and from the Banff Railway Station as well as around the Bow Valley on sightseeing excursions.

journey. Undertaken as either a vacation or, equally likely, as the shortest and most efficient route to Asia from Europe, such a trip was a popular if expensive venture. The idea appealed to Europeans with hereditary wealth, to the robber barons and the nouveau riche of North America, to princes, to politicians, to patrons of the arts, and even to the dour financiers of Eastern Canada.

Along the way, one could be assured of exchanging pleasantries and practising one-upmanships with the "proper" people, and it was to this end the hotel played its full hand. As one early visitor to Banff put it:

One who stays here for two hours realizes the distinction between "the man who lived in the terraced house and the brother in the streets below" . . . for one either stops at The Hotel, or he does not. There are several hotels—some on hillsides set in pleasant parks, others on the banks of the Bow River, and some on the main street of town—and then there is the Banff Springs Hotel.

The idea that the Banff Springs was *the* hotel began as soon as the guests alighted on Banff Railway Station's wooden boardwalk. There, they were confronted by a long line of carriage drivers and employees of the various hotels in town, each shouting out the name and virtues of his particular establishment. The din of the rival voices might at first give the traveller the impression that Banff was a large metropolis with the greatest array of deluxe accommodation on the continent. It did not take long, however, to sort through the confusion and realize that the carriage of the Banff Springs Hotel, by virtue of its size, platform position, and well-groomed team of four or six horses, was the obvious choice for those who were serious about their pleasures.

During the 20-minute carriage ride, guests were carried from the station through the Banff townsite and across the river to the great arcade of the hotel's courtyard, where visitors arriving by day caught their first glimpse of what life at the Banff Springs might offer:

"We tried both principal hotels, the Canadian Pacific and the Sanitarium; the former cost nearly double as much as the latter, but then it is a palace hotel."

– Douglas Sladen, 1895

In the courtyard are riding-horses and grooms in cowboy costumes, smoothly tailored women about to go for a climb in the mountains, and uniformed servants standing at the entrance eager to be of assistance to arriving or departing guests. It is a picture that one imagines exists only in reality at some medieval castle in Tyrol.

Inside, guests found all the latest conveniences, including electric lights, steam heat, and even an elevator for those too infirm or too dignified to climb two flights of stairs. The earliest guests paid $3.50 per night,

An 1896 winter outing, overseen by hotel manager Mathews in the back seat. Sleighs replaced tally-hos as the favoured means of transportation during the winter months.

which, at twice the cost of the other hotels in town, provided "a luxuriously furnished room, a private bath, and fare much the same as on an Atlantic liner"—everything, in fact, but the wine.

While one malcontent found the main dining room "not so good," reminiscent "of an Italian convent being turned into a barrack," others noted the smoothly tailored waiters and live chamber music and were disinclined to think of anything but the sensuous feast at hand:

You sit at dinner in style, and eat your fried chicken a la Maryland to the "March El Capitan" or a Fantaisie from Der Freischutz, played by the Melrose Trio—three clever young ladies who are great on the piano, the violin, and the seductive "cello". You look out on the mountains from any or every window, and are fetched back from a reverie by an American female at your table ordering green tea.

The musicians would also present concerts each evening after dinner, invariably causing the young to sentimentalize and the old to become retrospective. Other favourite after-dinner pastimes included a session in the bar and billiard room, where the affairs of the world—the discovery of gold in the Yukon, Laurier's new Liberal government, and the threat of colonial war in South Africa—might be put in order; a moonlight stroll down to the Bow Falls; and, for the European guests, a chat with the Americans,

The North-West Mounted Police "E" Division band at the Banff Springs Hotel, 1888.

a constant source of delight and amazement for the travel-journal set. The combination of American innocence and money proved irresistible to many British tourists who, as one historian suggested, "often went abroad with the air of landlords surveying their Empire." As one of these British tourists reported:

Some of [the Americans] are very plain people, and tell the story of how they became rich with much naiveté, disowning the idea of their possessing any special faculty (in which the hearer is disposed to agree with them) and confessing also that they don't know what to do with their money now they've got it, which also seems easily understandable.

Another watched a group of new arrivals from the United States look on in wonder as the British guests stood for the band's traditional 10:00 p.m. rendition of "God Save the Queen." In a misguided effort to transcribe an American drawl, he wrote:

"Wall," said one lady to another while waiting for the lift, "I think it was jest sweet of them Britishers. I've come into a foreign country, a long ways from home, and they played the American tune, 'My Country 'tis of Thee,' and all the Britishers stood. I cud hev jest cried with happiness!"

It would, of course, be wrong to assume that all the early guests were either stuffy British citizens exercising the entitlements of wealth or ingenuous Americans hell-bent on revealing their ignorance. One of the hotel's early frequenters who avoided both shortcomings was none other than Lady Agnes Macdonald, the wife of Canada's first prime minister. Lady Macdonald was a highly energetic woman who possessed a rare ability to balance cultural propriety, curiosity, and a great zest for life. Travelling with her husband on their first transcontinental trip in 1886, she was so inspired by the Rockies that she decided to abandon the confines of their private car and ride from "summit to sea" (Lake Louise to Vancouver) on the train's cowcatcher—the plow-shaped metal grille attached to the front of the locomotive that bumped animals off the tracks. While her husband dismissed the whole affair as "rather ridiculous," Lady Agnes was ecstatic: "There is glory of brightness and beauty everywhere, and I laugh aloud on the cowcatcher, just because it is all so delightful!"

Lady Agnes Macdonald

Lady Agnes became so enamoured of Banff during her 1886 trip that she had a private cabin built for her adjacent to the hotel. Naming the cottage the Earnscliffe, after the manor she lived in with her husband in Ottawa, she spent time there during the summers of 1887, '88, and '89, and thus would have witnessed the completion of the hotel and its first years of operation. She combined her love of word games and wood-carving by inscribing the cottage's fireplace mantel with *If the B m.t. put : it*, i.e., "If the grate be empty, put coal on it." The cottage, in a much-renovated form, still stands to the south of the hotel. It has served as a storage facility, a rental shop for snowmobiles, and, more recently, a comfortable residence for the hotel's managers.

Another early frequenter of the hotel, a nephew of George Stephen, was as interesting as Lady Macdonald, if for different reasons. He disliked hotel lobbies as much as Lady Agnes liked cowcatchers. He took all

George Stephen's eccentric nephew.

his meals in his room and used the room's window as an entrance and exit, preferring never to cross through the rotunda and use the hotel's main doors.

Another early guest of note, decidedly more sociable, was a young, good-looking, millionaire named Ross Thompson. Thompson was the embodiment of a Western rags-to-riches tale wherein a down-and-out itinerant jack-of-few-trades improbably converts a mining claim into a real estate bonanza. In the summer of 1896, with both wealth and reputation well in hand, he checked into the Banff Springs Hotel, ready to mix a little business with his pleasure.

Unbeknownst to the other guests, Thompson had been in Banff before, disastrously, in the summer of 1888. While bumming a train ride towards the British Columbia interior and his fortune, he was arrested for both wantonly disturbing the peace (convicted) and burglary (acquitted). Despite the passage of time, the humiliation still burned brightly when he returned eight years later.

Whatever Thompson's hopes for revenge might have been, they improved greatly when he discovered that a man named Stellarton—one of a group of New York financers who had earlier tried unsuccessfully to separate Thompson from his mining claim—was also registered at the hotel. Stellarton, aspiring to the select social circle of the "New York 400," was eager to meet Thompson, set things straight, and, not at all incidentally, introduce Thompson to his daughter. During his week at the hotel, Thompson was sociable with the other guests, struck up friendships with many of the townspeople, innocently courted Stellarton's daughter, and became friendly with Inspector Harper of the North-West Mounted Police. He was, he said, interested in police work.

On his final night in town, Thompson invited the Stellarton family and Inspector Harper to a private farewell dinner party. Arrangements with the head waiter ensured the wine glasses were full at all times, and while Thompson talked much and drank little, his guests talked little and drank much. At some point in the evening, Mrs. Stellarton disappeared under the table, and was subsequently carried to her room by Thompson and the hotel manager. Harper and Mr. Stellarton trailed not far behind, arm in arm, volubly discussing the possibility of a national US police force with Inspector Harper at the helm. Yet later in the evening, when Harper was finally loaded into the buggy waiting to carry him back to the barracks, Thompson asked the driver, a corporal in the force, to remind Harper to glance over the police charge sheet for 1888, when he awoke the next morning.

Within a day, the news of the dinner and the guests' antics had spread throughout the town. The Stellartons quickly decided they would spend the rest of their holidays in a spot where the snickers (many from behind the cuffs of the "400") weren't quite so pointed. Inspector Harper had no such option to depart, but one could assume he wished he might do the same.

While there were, no doubt, other intrigues hatched in the hotel, the major business of the day was simply recreation and pleasure. The only real pursuit was to stretch the body and spirit in the mountain sunshine and listen to the humming of one's own head in a wilderness silence that had yet to be broken by the racket of the "infernal" combustion engine.

It was, in fact, the wilderness environment that provided much of the hotel's character and set it apart from other fine hotels in more civilized places. For while it was possible to listen to Liszt's Rhapsody No. 2 on a new Steinway piano in the evening ("a treat hardly to be expected in the middle of the Rockies"), the daytime hours presented a mad swirl of outdoor activity. Packers such as Tom Wilson, George Fear, and Bill and Jim Brewster started their businesses in the hotel's early years, and the era of men such as "Wild Bill" Peyto and Jimmy Simpson was close at hand. The CPR-imported Swiss guides were never far away, ever ready to take hotel guests to nearby summits. All in all, the various mountain men and the exotic paraphernalia of their respective trades marked a colourful, energizing contrast to the world of 19th-century propriety, and most of the guests were willing to exchange the formality of Eastern dress for a pair of sturdy outdoor boots.

Taking a cruise aboard the Mountain Belle *on the Bow River was a popular activity for early hotel guests.*

THREE FOR THE MOUNTAINS

The guides and outfitters of early Banff occupy a cherished spot in a history filled with larger-than-life characters and legendary exploits. Among their number, three stand out: Thomas Edmonds Wilson, Ebenezer William "Wild Bill" Peyto, and Justin James McCartney Simpson. All of them looked to the Banff Springs for clients, and all worked to organize, supply, and guide trips ranging from a few days in the wilderness around Banff to the entire summer into remote corners of the Canadian Rockies. Their clients were a mixed lot, interested in sight-seeing, science, surveying and mapping, fishing, hunting, climbing, photography, and painting. Adventure was the common denominator.

Tom Wilson

Tom Wilson, early Banff's premier guide and outfitter, left his Ontario home in 1859 at age 16 with a desire to see the West. After a stint with the North-West Mounted Police, he was hired as a packer for the CPR mountain survey. The work gave him a detailed knowledge of a landscape that was still largely unknown to non-Indigenous people. Among other "firsts," he is famous for being the first European to visit the "Lake of the Little Fishes," now Lake Louise.

Wilson's experience left him well positioned to set up his own business when a market for wilderness travel emerged. Advertising himself as "Guide to the CPR," he was soon hiring other outfitters to help meet the demand for his services. Working for alpinists, sportsmen, and tourist-explorers, he led pioneering journeys to Mount Assiniboine, the headwaters of the North Saskatchewan River and the Yoho Valley.

One of the best-known Wilson stories recounts his 121-kilometre (75-mile) snowshoe trip from his winter ranch on the North Saskatchewan River to Banff in 1908. Wishing to join his family for Christmas dinner, he set out on what turned into a multiday epic journey through the teeth of a Canadian Rockies blizzard. During the trip, he froze his feet after falling through a snow bridge, fought for three days through heavy snow on a broken snowshoe and with no food, and resisted the urge to just give up and go to sleep. "It would have been so much easier to quit than go on," he said. But go on he did. With characteristic dry humour, he later claimed, "The pleasure of the meal was well worth the trip."

As a living part of Banff's greatest era of exploration, discovery, and adventure, it was fitting that Wilson spent his final years—until his death in 1933—working once more for the CPR, this time entertaining guests at the Banff Springs with stories from "the old days" in the Rockies.

"Wild Bill" Peyto arrived in the Rockies from England in 1887. After working for the CPR in British Columbia and homesteading near Cochrane, he went prospecting in the Bow Valley and met Tom Wilson. Signing on as a Wilson trailhand, Peyto proved to be a good guide and packer, described by one client as

Bill Peyto

"efficient, highly imaginative, an excellent man with the horses and a good friend." Guiding a number of exploratory trips north of Lake Louise along what is today the Icefields Parkway, he played an important role in the discovery of the Columbia Icefield. Peyto Lake and Peyto Glacier are named in his honour.

Although Peyto was a solitary person of few words, he looked like the quintessential mountain man and was willing to play the part. He had blue eyes so piercing they could reputedly turn back a grizzly, and his standard trail garb included tattered trousers, a sombrero, a fringed buckskin coat, a heavy cartridge belt, a revolver, and a hunting knife. He once lived up to his "Wild Bill" moniker by strolling down Banff Avenue and into a local bar with a live trapped lynx slung across his back. Spotting some miners he disliked, he released the lynx and stood back to enjoy the show.

Peyto's career as an outfitter was relatively brief, perhaps in part because guiding required too much interaction with strangers. After a turn at trapping and prospecting, he became a park warden in 1913. The work suited him, and with the exception of a term of service in the Great War, he stayed with the park until his retirement in 1936. He continued to live in Banff until his death in 1943.

Jimmy Simpson, the "Grand Old Man of the Mountains," was born in England in 1877. He was bright lad but mischievous, and his family, tiring of his antics, gave him a small remittance and packed him off to Canada. Travelling west, Simpson eventually found work as a trail cook for Wilson and met Bill Peyto, who became his role model and mentor. "I wanted to be like Peyto," he declared. "Or die in the attempt."

In time, Simpson earned a reputation as a congenial and talented guide. Among other skills, he was so adept on snowshoes that the Stoneys named him "Nashan-esen" ("wolverine-go-quick"). He started his own business in Banff with an outlying camp at Bow Lake, north of Lake Louise, and it was there he later built Num-ti-jah Lodge, catering to tourists who by then were travelling north by car.

In his later years, Simpson lived in a small cabin at the lodge where he painted, tended to his beloved horses, and visited with friends. He died at the age of 95, in 1972. While reminiscing shortly before his death, he smiled, caught in the memories of distant times, and said, "Banff was a *real* place back then."

Jimmy Simpson

Canoeing on the Bow River, strolling down to Bow Falls, taking a pleasure cruise up the Bow on the *Mountain Belle*, or renting horses or a tally-ho for a ride out to the Hoodoos or Lake Minnewanka were favourite pastimes. Fishing was an openly competitive event—guests vied with each other for the greatest poundage. In one case, the competition went so far as to spur one party into stuffing its best effort with rocks, a ploy discovered and decried back at the hotel when some impudent noncompetitor dared to observe that the fish's mouth had been sewn shut.

> *"The hot springs . . . combined with the great glaciers and magnificent mountain scenery, are drawing a large number of visitors, the more enthusiastic of whom declare that Banff is the most beautiful spot in the world."*
>
> – *Dominion Illustrated*, 1888

The Canadian Rockies' numerous virgin peaks offered yet another sort of sport. Many famous European climbers, finding the number of unclimbed mountains in the Alps rapidly diminishing, were drawn to Western Canada by the thought of whole mountain ranges yet to be named, let alone climbed. For example, Edward Whymper, conqueror of the Matterhorn and one of the elite members of the British Alpine Club—launched in 1857 as the first organization in the world to promote the new sport of mountaineering—organized his first outing in the Canadian Rockies at the Banff Springs Hotel, although not without difficulty. The esteemed alpinist was one of the crustier specimens of the upper crust, and he viewed the local packers as a subspecies. It was only after hotel manager Mathews took him aside and explained that Canadians, too, considered themselves to be card-carrying members of the human race that Whymper humbled himself enough to engage Bill Peyto as a guide and packer for his first trip.

The hot springs were of course another major draw. Indeed, according to one source, the hotel was named the "Banff Springs" to highlight its proximity to the "hot sulphurous water gushing from the earth for the hypochondriacs to drink, and the halt, lame, and withered to bathe in as well." The hotel's plunge pool and 10 private baths were popular with all the guests, including those in the pink of health, but particularly so with those who believed they would benefit from the waters' curative powers. As publicized, the springs were "especially efficacious for the cure of rheumatic, gouty, and allied conditions," as well as for

Climbing was a major draw for European alpinists, many of whom based themselves at the Banff Springs Hotel.

William Fear and Tom Wilson outside their Banff Avenue store in 1896.

conditions of "the liver, diabetes, Bright's disease and chronic dyspepsia."

The water was piped down from the Upper Hot Springs, located above the hotel on the side of Sulphur Mountain. Various plumbing problems often resulted in such a reduced flow of water that little if any reached the hotel's pool, and at such times the hotel staff would surreptitiously fill the pool with hot water and dump in bags of sulphur. This worked tolerably well until the water once again flowed from the springs proper.

All told, there was no lack of things to do, either at the hotel or in its immediate environs. Although the Banff Springs couldn't claim any such bear stories as the one boasted by the rival Sanitarium Hotel—in which Sergeant Casey Oliver's pet bear wandered into the hotel one night and climbed into bed with an unsuspecting guest—it could never be said that any of its early guests expired from boredom.

The hotel and its traffic were bound to have an effect on "the man in the streets below," and the little town of Banff was as quick to capitalize the tourist as Van Horne had been to capitalize the scenery. By 1900, Banff Avenue was bustling with small shops, restaurants, hotels, and other businesses. Guides and packers were busy with backcountry clients, and a whole service industry had developed around the needs of the "halt, lame, and withered" who came to cast aside their crutches at the various hot springs establishments. The Banff Springs—

which was the largest hotel, entertained the wealthiest clientele, and had the CPR's resources to lure yet more people to the area—played a critical role in Banff's economy. "The Banff Springs," one resident said, "was Banff's bread and butter."

While most visitors found the townspeople to be a congenial sort, there was some grumbling that the town had been oversold and that the business community was overly convinced of its own importance. As one of the travel-journal set complained in 1895:

Not that the town of Banff has much to boast of. It has a few hundred inhabitants, who have succeeded in making the surrounding woods and mountains more destitute of bird and beast and flower than a Park at Montreal. Though it consists of but a single street, it is horribly over civilized. It has even a chemist, from whom, as far back as three or four years ago, you could buy Kipling's books in the unauthorised editions.

Destitution, overcivilization, and Kipling's books to the contrary, the town had a good heart. Young Ross Thompson, on his first unfortunate journey through Banff, was given a gift of cheese and bread, no questions asked, by an old French grocer. Thompson didn't forget the act his second time in town. On that occasion, he managed to visit "Frenchy" once each day; he'd buy a bit of candy for the grocer's children and pay for it with a five-dollar gold piece.

The town was also able to overlook aspersions cast from the "castle on the hill." In later years, the hotel's "snob element" would rankle some of the community's aspiring socialites, just as the hotel's railway station platform privileges would rankle the owners of other hotels, but by and large, the town took pride in the hotel. An article in an early issue of the local paper, after describing the beauties of the building, grants it immunity from the world of finance: "It does no[t] seem fit that one should go into detail on the money or the toil it has cost to bring this incomparable institution to its present stage of perfection. Mercenary ideas jar the romance of the situation."

Despite the townspeople's support for the hotel and their dependence on it for a portion of their meal ticket, few of them ever saw the inside of the building. Most, in fact, were only vaguely aware of the elegance that lay behind the great carved doors. It was "a palace unto itself," and most of the local populace would never consider transgressing its glittering domain. The concept of social class was a vigorous doctrine at the turn of the century, and it kept the "downtown people" downtown.

Some annual social events brought the hotel and the town together, though. One was the hotel summer ball, which allowed the established families of Banff and Calgary brief but heady access to the sequestered social registers of New York and Boston. Lucky local guests could later speak in casual tones of mingling with European and Eastern royalty.

Another was Banff Indian Days, which brought hotel clients, townspeople, and members of the Stoney Nakoda First Nation together for a multiday cultural festival. Beginning in 1894, when flooding in British Columbia washed out sections of the CPR and the hotel manager was left scrambling for ways to entertain his stranded guests, the gathering evolved into one of Banff's most popular annual events.

There were other, more mundane, points of connection. One concern that troubled both Banff and the hotel was that of the penniless transient, a problem that has dogged the sensibilities of a certain class of Banffites since the settlement's earliest days. The transient of 1900 took one of two forms: the common hobo, aka the boxcar bum, or the gentleman thief, who would ride the train legitimately, strike up an acquaintance with wealthy travellers, and then steal from them as much of whatever was convenient when the opportunity arose.

Both types were anathema to the town. A news article entitled "The Tramp Nuisance Infesting our Mountain Resorts" decried the presence of such individuals: "They must be taught that these sylvan retreats, though free to the world, must be kept absolutely free if not from their presence at any rate from their outrages." At one point, the possibility of gentlemen thieves operating at the Banff Springs prompted manager Mathews to ask guests to keep a close eye on their possessions. For all its splendour, resources, and elevated position, the Banff Springs remained part and parcel of the larger community below.

BANFF INDIAN DAYS

For almost 90 years, one of Banff's largest and most celebrated summer events was Banff Indian Days. The tradition began in 1894, after floods from a heavy winter snowpack washed out several railway bridges in British Columbia and thus halted CPR traffic through the province for much of June and July. Banff, suddenly finding itself the end of the line for westbound traffic, was left to accommodate a multitude of stranded passengers.

Trying to come up with new entertainments for his marooned guests, Banff Springs Hotel manager W. L. Mathews asked outfitter Tom Wilson to approach the nearby Stoney Nakoda community about showcasing Stoney culture at the hotel. The resulting event proved so popular with hotel visitors, townsfolk, and Stoney participants alike that it became an annual affair.

The festival opened with a parade featuring Stoneys in full ceremonial dress on horseback. Starting northeast of the townsite, the procession moved south along Banff Avenue and across the Bow River, and ended in the Banff Springs' courtyard. The parade marked the beginning of several days of singing, dancing, and athletic competitions, including horse racing.

While the last Banff Indian Days was held in 1978, the Stoneys reinstituted an annual return to the Indian Grounds in 2004. The more recent gatherings, however, happen for very different reasons than those that propelled Indian Days. Today, the event is a low-key, private gathering in which cultural traditions are honoured, renewed, and passed on to a younger generation of the Stoney Nakoda First Nation.

Banff Indian Days, 1894, with Chief Hector Crawler (centre) and Tom Wilson (to his right).

A sightseeing carriage departing the Banff Springs Hotel, 1908.

Growing Pains

"THE RECORD OF MEALS SERVED PER MONTH AT THE HOTEL HAS EXCEEDED BY 2,000 THE FIGURE OF THE GREAT SEATTLE FAIR SEASON OF TWO YEARS AGO."

By the beginning of the 20th century, it was apparent that Van Horne's scheme to build a string of grand mountain hotels had been a stroke of genius. Within 12 years of its opening, the Banff Springs Hotel had become one of the top mountain resorts in North America, had established a solid international reputation, and was proving to be a lucrative venture for the Canadian Pacific Railway. The 1894 *Baedeker's Canada* listed it alongside other top hotels in the Dominion, the others being the Château Frontenac in Quebec, Windsor Station in Montreal, and Russell House and Grand

"The only business at Banff is to enjoy one's self, to recreate, to loaf in the sunshine and worship nature."
– Bernard McEvoy, 1902

A 1905 Banff Springs Hotel postcard.

CANADA'S OTHER RAILWAY HOTELS

Enticing passengers to stay in company-owned hotels was one of the CPR's early marketing objectives. Under the leadership of visionaries, such as Van Horne, hotels were constructed in prominent cities and the remote wilderness was penetrated by the transcontinental line. Competing railways such as the Grand Trunk Pacific Railway and Canadian National Railway followed suit. The result was a string of grand hotels stretching from coast to coast. They attracted wealthy guests from around the world and formed an important piece of Canada's national identity.

The Algonquin (St. Andrews, New Brunswick): Opened in 1889, and now known as the Algonquin Resort, this sprawling waterfront lodge was built near Van Horne's summer home.

Algonquin Resort opened in 1889.

Château Champlain (Montreal, Quebec): Opened in 1967 for the World's Fair, the former CPR hotel with its distinctive porthole windows is now the part of the Marriott chain.

Château Frontenac (Quebec City, Quebec): Designed by Banff Springs architect Bruce Price and opened in 1894, the internationally famous hotel was recognized as a National Historic Site in 1980. It now operates as the Fairmont Le Château Frontenac.

Château Lake Louise (Banff National Park, Alberta): Originally a small log chalet built by the CPR in 1890, the château was rebuilt in the 1920s and is today one of the world's most photographed hotels.

The CPR constructed a chalet at Lake Louise in 1890.

Château Laurier (Ottawa, Ontario): Opened in 1912 in downtown Ottawa close to Parliament Hill, today's Fairmont Château Laurier is a famous political hotspot.

Château Montebello (Montebello, Quebec): Opened in 1930 as the world's largest log hotel, it is today the Fairmont Le Château Montebello.

The Empress (Victoria, British Columbia): Overlooking Victoria's Inner Harbour, the city's most famous Edwardian landmark is now the Fairmont Empress.

The Fort Garry (Winnipeg, Manitoba): A classic 1913 château-style railway hotel, the Fort Garry, like the Banff Springs and the Château Frontenac, is now a National Historic Site of Canada.

Glacier House (Glacier National Park, British Columbia): One of Van Horne's three original railway dining stations, Glacier House opened in 1886 and flourished as an important international mountaineering centre for many years. It closed in 1925.

Hotel Macdonald (Edmonton, Alberta): Another of the classic château-style hotels, Hotel Macdonald was built in 1914, saved from demolition in the 1980s, and is now a treasured part of the Fairmont family.

Hotel Nova Scotian (Halifax, Nova Scotia): Blending colonial and neoclassical styles, the former Canadian National Railway hotel, built in 1928, is now part of the Westin chain.

Hotel Saskatchewan (Regina, Saskatchewan): Opened by the CPR in 1927, the neoclassical downtown building is the city's finest hotel. It is now part of the Marriott chain.

Hotel Vancouver (Vancouver, British Columbia): Famous for its copper roof, the 1939 landmark is today the Fairmont Hotel Vancouver.

Jasper Park Lodge (Jasper, Alberta): Originally a row of lakeside tents operated by the Grand Trunk Pacific Railway, Jasper Park Lodge is today an upscale resort operated by Fairmont.

Minaki Lodge (Minaki, Ontario): Built along the Canadian National line in 1914 and then rebuilt in 1927, the resort-style granite-and-log hotel was subject to a succession of owners before burning to the ground in 2003.

Mount Stephen House (Yoho National Park, British Columbia): Another of Van Horne's original dining stations, Mount Stephen House opened in 1886 and, owing to demand, was quickly expanded to become a hotel. The structure was demolished in 1963.

Palliser Hotel (Calgary, Alberta): Opening in 1914, the landmark Palliser was the first CPR hotel to abandon the château style in favour of a neoclassical design. It is now part of the Fairmont chain.

Place Viger Hotel (Montreal, Quebec): Designed by Banff Springs architect Bruce Price, the combination railway station and hotel opened in 1898. Closed in 1935 when the station was moved, the hotel (and its accompanying property) has been the subject of many redevelopment plans. Currently it is a major commercial space anchored by Montreal tech company Lightspeed.

Queen Elizabeth Hotel (Montreal, Quebec): A large landmark hotel with over 1,000 rooms, the Queen Elizabeth was opened in 1958 and is now operated under the Fairmont brand.

Royal York Hotel (Toronto, Ontario): Opened in 1929, the Royal York became the flagship of the CPR city hotels. It is now the Fairmont Royal York.

Mount Stephen House, Field, around 1910.

In 1903, a new wing was completed on the south side of the original hotel.

Union in Ottawa. The Banff Springs was particularly noted in the guide for its "good cuisine and attendance."

Van Horne had stepped up to the position of CPR board chair, and it must have been a source of pride for him to see requests for hotel additions and improvements flow across the large, polished oak desks of the company's headquarters in Montreal. Such requests were not a small matter. The CPR hotels were having trouble keeping up with the demand for their services, and the Banff Springs in particular was experiencing outright cramping. The Rocky Mountains Park superintendent's reports to Ottawa for the years 1902–1905 reveal the pressure the hotel was under: in 1902, hotel guests numbered 3,890; the following year, the number jumped to 5,303; and in 1904, it nearly doubled, to 9,684. The reports also indicate that during each of those years, large numbers of guests were turned away due to lack of accommodation.

The Banff Springs Register, which the park superintendent considered some of the best reading in Banff in 1905, showed, on one page, names from South Africa, The Hague, Paris, Austria, England, Japan, Canada, the US, Borneo, and Hong Kong.

To meet the demands of an expanding international clientele, the CPR started a program of hotel extension and improvement that resulted in an addition or a rearrangement in the Banff Springs' structure almost every year between 1900 and 1928. The 28-year span is neatly divided into two periods: 1900 to 1910, during which all modifications dealt directly with the original 1888 building, and 1910 to

1928, during which the modifications were directed towards the ultimate end of a "new" hotel.

Exact dates and figures concerning additions, upgrades, and refurbishments between 1900 and 1910 are few and far between. The superintendent's reports do show, however, that the CPR allocated a half-million dollars—an amount roughly double the cost of the original hotel's construction—for construction and refurnishing in 1902 and that large projects were undertaken in 1903, 1904, and 1905. An extensive expansion occurred over the winter of 1902–03, when a crew worked to duplicate the original structure's west wing. The new wing, joined to the old by a low split-level passageway, was in essence a southern extension of the wing it duplicated. The result was the basic north-south orientation the hotel has maintained ever since.

The hotel's new appearance created a local journalistic furor. A news clipping from 1903 claimed that one could march an army of 3,000 men into the building. The reporter envisioned soldiers five abreast swinging through the south doors and marching down the main hall, leaving still enough room for an officer to "pass up and down the line without being crowded to the wall." Considering the commotion caused some years later when an inebriated park warden rode his horse into the lobby, it's just as well that no one tried to verify the accuracy of the journalist's claim. It's safe to assume, though, that Manager Mathews was content in the fact that his hotel could now house two-thirds again as many as the first hotel's 300 guests. (Incidentally, the closest thing to an army to ever reach the hotel was the celebrated 56th Regiment Iowa National Guard Band of Fort Dodge, Iowa, which was a great hit at the 1908 summer ball.)

This hand-tinted 1910 postcard shows visitors loading into a tally-ho at the new Banff Railway Station.

As for the interior renovations, it appears that management continued the hotel's previous motif:

It is finished in native wood—Douglas fir—every piece of which has gone through the hands of artistic wood workers. The ceiling and other decorations have been put on in accord with perfect harmony, and the electric lights—well, thousands have been spent on them. The parlours, the sleeping rooms, retreats, refreshment booths, verandas, baths, and all such are modern and luxurious to the limit.

The 1903 season also witnessed the installation of a complete set of telephones in the hotel. Earlier, the hotel had owned one of only four telephones in Banff, which bragged of being one of the earliest "wired" towns in the West. But even with a new wing, a new interior, and the convenience of telephones, the hotel could no more accommodate the number of guests desiring rooms in 1903 than it could in 1902. The park superintendent's report summarizes the problem:

No less than 5,000 guests were turned away from Banff during the past season. The Banff Springs Hotel was compelled to remain open for a month later than usual owing to its increasing popularity among the travelling public. Notwithstanding the large additions made to the building in 1903, which includes the addition of over 200 rooms, the management has since found it necessary to make arrangements for yet another large addition.

Interestingly, the proposed addition was to be built "with a view to being utilized throughout the winter." The "winter view" was common in Banff from 1900 until well into the 1920s, with merchants claiming that

Sometime before 1910, six-storey towers were added to the south and north wings.

each succeeding winter would be the winter that would establish Banff as a major winter resort. Obviously, the Banff Springs Hotel was not immune to such speculative possibilities, and progressive generations of managers toyed with the idea of making the hotel a year-round resort. But it wasn't until 1969 that the hotel finally opened for the winter.

The exact nature of the additions of 1904 and 1905 is not known, but it is possible they included capping the ends of the north and south wings with six-storey frame towers. With their steep-hipped and dormered roofs, the towers bore a strong resemblance to the ones that occupy similar positions today. If the towers did in fact go up in '04 or '05, it is more than likely that one of the first guests to enjoy their elevated view was Joseph Cannon, the long-time Speaker of the US House of Representatives. Cannon checked into the hotel during the 1905 season with a large retinue of fellow legislators and their wives, and one wonders what "Uncle Joe," who once vowed that the US House would spend "not one cent for scenery," thought of the Canadian Rockies.

In 1906, another "comfort and convenience" was added to the growing list of Banff Springs' amenities when six arc lights were installed along the road to the hotel. The installation report doesn't include how the townspeople reacted to the new technological marvel, but it does note the job was more complicated than necessary owing to six Italians on the crew who spoke no English.

The alterations continued during the winter of 1906–07, when a crew of some 70 men worked almost continuously to build a new boiler, engine, and laundry room. The new addition, at the southeast end of the hotel, was considered unique. Constructed entirely of river boulders and featuring a 90-foot smokestack, it prompted one journalist to predict, correctly, that it would be "recorded on many hundreds of photographic films before the season [was] over."

The only thing that outpaced construction during the first decade of the 20th century was, as in previous years, the number of people wanting to use the construction. When the hotel opened in May 1907, it was promptly filled to capacity with 450 registered guests, the start of another overflow season. The trend continued in 1908 and 1909, and during the summer of 1910, the hotel

THE BANFF SPRINGS HOTEL IN FICTION

The earliest reference to the Banff Springs Hotel in fiction appears in a 1910 novel, *Lady Merton, Colonist*, by Mrs. Humphry Ward, aka Mary Augusta Ward CBE. Mrs. Ward was well-known not only as a novelist but also as the founding president of the Women's National Anti-Suffrage League.

Lady Merton, Colonist is a story of adventure and romantic intrigue that follows the travels of an English widow and her ailing brother along the transcontinental railway through the wilds of Canada. The reference to the hotel consists of a flowery description of the view from the terrace:

The hotel at Banff overlooks a wide scene of alp and water. The splendid Bow River comes swirling past the hotel, on its rush from the high mountains to the plains of Saskatchewan. Craggy mountains drop almost to the river's edge on one side; on the other, pine woods mask the railway and the hills; while in the distance shine the snow-peaks of the Rockies.

Tourists in tally-ho viewing the buffalo in the animal enclosure, which was at the base of Cascade Mountain, 1910.

sent close to 400 people back to the railway station to find shelter in sleeping cars at $1.50 per night. During that summer, the hotel entertained at least two parties noteworthy of the local paper: a convention of over 100 businessmen from Winnipeg, and the maharaja of Baroda, accompanied by the maharani, their two children, and an entourage of friends and servants.

> *"What is the difference between this hotel and the C.P.R.?" asked a grouchy gest at the King Edward recently. "Just a mile, sir" was Tabby's reply, and the humour of it dispelled the grouch."*
>
> *– Crag and Canyon*, 1907

The supply and demand issue continued unabated into 1911. Well over 22,000 people stayed at the hotel during the summer, and it was noted that "the record of meals served per month at the hotel has exceeded by 2,000 the figure of the great Seattle fair season of two years ago."

Aside from two or three dances a week, tennis courts that were full to overflowing every day the weather permitted, and inevitable sightseeing, the guests of 1911 were able to enjoy a brand new entertainment: a nine-hole golf course designed by Scotsman William Thomson. The course took full advantage of the mountain setting, winding its way along the Bow River on an ancient alluvial fan. Hole lengths ranged from 160 to 500 yards, and guests paid $0.50 a round or $1.00 per day to enjoy the spectacular fairways. The course was a hit—some 1,500 guests played the new links in the nine weeks following its opening—and a new, enduring Banff Springs' legacy was born. A local club member, Don Matheson, conveyed some of the excitement of local enthusiasts as well as the arcane jargon of the game as then played in his review:

The course is not to the strong so much as to the strong mid-iron player, their mid-iron being potentially worth two brassies from the utilitarian point of view. The iron in the hands of a player who can save a stroke on the green with his mashie shot, is mightier than the driver and the baffy combined; and less conducive to the development of the sin of execration than a foozle with a cleek in cuppy lie.

Local paper the *Crag & Canyon*, in its article on the course's opening, called it "a capital addition to the attractions of the Park."

While the folks downtown fulminated about the growing number of "roughs" in town—the "class of visitor who make the Banff trip as an excuse for a glorious drunk"—the Banff Springs was worrying much less about the quality of its clientele than the quantity of the clientele it could accommodate. The mountain scenery, indeed, had been capitalized.

Banff Springs Golf Course, 1915.

Workers quarrying limestone for the new hotel.

Towers and Troubles

"THE CHATEAUX OF THE LOIRE . . . OR IS IT EARLY WILLIAM RANDOLPH HEARST?"

By 1910, it was apparent the piecemeal approach to construction that the hotel had pursued for the previous decade would not solve the institution's capacity problems. Furthermore, the staggering headcount for the 1910 and 1911 seasons, including the people who had bedded down at the railway station, emphasized the point that the hotel's potential was not being fulfilled. The CPR barons of Montreal bent their greying temples together and announced what appeared to be a simple answer—begin work on a new Banff Springs Hotel. And if the old hotel had been the "largest and finest mountain resort on the continent," the new hotel would be larger and finer yet.

It isn't known if the planners of 1910 envisioned a completely new structure, one to be built in stages over a number of years, or merely a greatly modified and integrated structure involving the old components. In either case, their decision to significantly alter the hotel's appearance and create something "new" was the key element in the evolution of the building that, with some later modifications, constitutes the core of today's hotel.

The man commissioned to design the new hotel was Walter S. Painter, an American who had been working as the chief architect for the Canadian Pacific Railway since 1905. Painter was acquainted with Banff and the Banff Springs Hotel at the time of the commission, having visited the community in the years before 1911. It seems likely that he was directly involved with much of the Banff Springs' renovation between 1903 and 1911. He obviously had a deep affinity for the hotel and for Banff, where he retired in 1957.

As an architect, Painter was influenced by both Price's work and the CPR's château tradition as a whole, and he would prove himself an able successor to Price. The CPR had begun to stray from the château style by 1910, especially in its designs for city hotels (such as Calgary's neoclassical Palliser Hotel), but the château was still considered appropriate for mountain resorts. Accordingly, Painter was treated to an extensive tour of the Loire region of France before he began drawing up plans for the new Banff Springs Hotel.

Walter S. Painter, architect of the new hotel.

Painter's trip to the Loire posed an intriguing question. Why, after spending his summer studying and sketching superb examples of the unadulterated French château, did Painter come home to build a structure that lacked most of the features that characterize the French medieval style? The dormers of the

Painter's 1911 sketch for a "new" Banff Springs Hotel. Only the centre tower, however, was completed as sketched.

present hotel are flat (rather than pointed); the arches are circular (rather than pointed); and the windows of the centre tower are rounded. All of these features are more indicative of the Scots baronial tradition than of the pure French château.

The question has at least two answers. The Scots baronial style of the 16th and 17th centuries was heavily influenced by the Loire châteaux, and Painter was probably interested in seeing the original source material. As well, the CPR was anxious to exploit the well-nurtured misconception that the Banff of the Canadian Rockies somehow resembled Banffshire in Scotland. This latter theme has played an important part in the projected image of Banff and the Banff Springs Hotel since the turn of the 20th century, and it has even been speculated that Price's original 1888 structure was designed with a Scottish manse in mind. This is doubtful, though, and, besides, the original building was much too loose a structure to allow such architectural pinpointing.

In any event, the hotel, as finished in 1928, owes much to both the French and Scottish styles but constitutes an exact copy of neither. Nor is it, as one visitor suggested, "early William Randolph Hearst." It is, as was the original hotel, its own building, diverse in influence and rich in design.

The first step in the creation of the new building was taken shortly after the hotel closed at the end of the 1911 season. A crew of some 200 men started tearing out the old centre portion of the hotel and preparing foundations for a new reinforced-concrete middle wing. The new wing was to become part of an 11-storey centre tower, given advanced billing as the tallest building in the Canadian Rockies.

But most of the work that first winter went towards completing the centre wing and developing two new swimming pools and a series of bathing rooms. The number of men on the job, many of them brought to town by the CPR, gave Banff its "finest winter to date," and the local paper reported happily that the winter sports club and the hockey club were active all winter long. The influx of men also created the first recorded housing shortage in Banff.

The work on the wing and the pools was completed by the early spring of 1912, and the results fully supported the assertion that the new structure would be a grand affair. The pools and baths were particularly impressive. A Calgary newspaper reported that the Banff Springs opened the season with "the finest bathing establishment on the continent," while the *Crag & Canyon* mentioned a "general air of luxury" about the place.

The "bathing establishment" consisted of three stacked terraces. The outer and lower terrace consisted of a semicircular cold freshwater pool. Above it, the second terrace sported a warm sulphur pool, heated to 43 degrees Celsius (109 degrees Fahrenheit) and separated from the outer freshwater pool by a graceful open-sided arcade. The second terrace also included Turkish and Russian baths with no fewer than 100 individual dressing rooms. The Turkish baths, with partitions of marble and walls and floors of imported English tile, proved to be the most popular. They were, wrote a local journalist, "quite the best part of the Dominion." The third terrace, with a roof that functioned as a wide promenade and viewing platform, included a number of cooling rooms, private sulphur baths, and massage rooms complete with a Swedish masseur.

One of the first people to enjoy the new baths was none other than the Duke of Connaught. The duke (brother of King Edward) and duchess (Princess Louise Margaret of Prussia) stopped briefly at the hotel on their first Canadian transcontinental journey, and the duke promised to return, saying, "[M]y only regret is that I have so short a time to enjoy the many attractions which are presented by Banff and its vicinities."

Although construction was halted for the duration of the 1912 season, by mid-September the cacophony associated with heavy construction could again be heard above the roar of the Bow Falls. A crew even larger than that of 1911 was employed for the winter work of 1912. Some estimates say there were as many as 600 men, although it is doubtful that there were ever more than 400 on the job at any one time.

The task for the next two winters was clear: build the tallest building in the Canadian Rockies before the start of the 1914 season. Walter Painter undertook the contract himself and promised to complete the work on time, a task most people considered impossible.

The building process was slow, arduous, and dramatic. Most of the labour was done by hand, and the men had access to none of the mechanical devices that help modern contractors toss up a 20-storey high-rise in a few months. Tons of materials were hauled by wagon from the railway station to the building site and then pushed and pulled into position by the builders' brute force. Elaborate scaffolding, the construction of which seemed nearly as impressive as the work on the hotel itself, was first erected and then enclosed in planks to protect the men from frigid winter winds and snow that seemed at times to rise more quickly than the tower. But the work did progress, and in 13 months the hotel manager was able to announce that the "alterations" were almost complete. Painter, it appeared, would make his contract.

Work on the centre tower nears completion in 1914.

Including the whole of the centre wing, the Painter Tower (more frequently called the "centre tower" today) is 60 metres (197 feet) long, 21 metres (69 feet) wide, and 11 storeys high—and its construction represents a remarkable achievement given the times and working conditions. It is even more remarkable that during the entire course of construction only two architectural mishaps occurred, neither of which were as grave as the about-face of the hotel's blueprint in 1888. The first problem was that the tower's east wall fell out of plumb early in its construction. The error wasn't discovered until the building had reached some five or six storeys, by which time it was too late to start over. Fortunately, the off-kilter angle was small. A mid-course correction was made, and the building continued its ascent without further incident. (The correction is still visible today, but visitors have to look hard to find it.)

The other blunder was revealed much later, when the building was nearing completion. One of the construction foremen called a joiner named Sam Ward over to him, and, pointing to one of the high dormered windows, asked if Ward remembered anything about the room behind the window. Ward didn't, and when the two investigated, they found nothing but a smooth, finished wall where there should have been a door. Sam found a pry bar and, while the foreman flinched, drove it between the studs to reveal a room that had been totally sealed off.

Nearly everyone agreed that the work on the new tower was generally superb, but if any one element drew universal acclaim it was the stonework. The CPR, to do things properly, had imported Italian stonecutters and Scottish masons, reputedly the best in the world at their respective jobs, to handle the tower's rock facing.

The rock itself is Rundlestone, a sedimentary limestone that was quarried from beside the Spray River, one kilometre upstream from the hotel. Once quarried, the rock was hauled by wagon to the building site, where the masons did the final shaping and laying of the blocks. The rock splits and breaks easily, which made the job a tedious one. But the cutters and masons proved equal to their reputations. As an observant guest might notice today, the centre tower's rockwork is of the highest quality—better than the work done in later years on other additions. Indeed, the earlier work is of a consistency and quality that likely couldn't be duplicated today.

Another interesting element of the Painter Tower is the great chunk of bedrock that is an integral part of the tower's northern wall. (It can be seen today where the tower joins the hotel's north wing outside the Rundle Lounge.) It was, of course, an architectural decision to incorporate the bedrock into the wall, probably to avoid the effort of knocking out a particularly resistant piece of rock and, perhaps, to add an ornamental and definitely organic touch to the structure. One other piece of bedrock, considerably larger, was never excavated from the hotel's subbasement. It was simply walled off, and one would suppose it became a robust support for the floors above it.

The Painter Tower was ready for business when the hotel opened in May 1914. Over two million dollars had been spent on the tower and a new interior, which now emphasized wicker furniture, imported red English tile, and dark wainscoting. The

RUGGED RUNDLESTONE

The hotel's exterior is faced with Rundlestone, a locally quarried rock distinctive for its rugged appearance and deep-grey, black, and brown hues. Geologically, it is sedimentary shale that originated as layers of sand deposited 250 million years ago on an ancient ocean floor. Such early marine origins account for the sea fossils found within the rock, a presence that continues to surprise visitors in a place so far from any ocean. The rock used for early iterations of the hotel was excavated from the base of Mount Rundle, at a quarry that can still be seen from the Spray River hiking trail. The rock that graces the hotel's more recent renovations and additions was excavated east of Banff at a quarry near Canmore. The rock remains a popular local building material and is commonly seen in

Looking down the Spray River to the hotel from the original quarry.

fireplaces, rock gardens, and interior floors throughout the mountain towns of Banff and Canmore, and beyond.

interior was the work of Kate Reed. The wife of a CPR executive, Reed was a talented decorator and was responsible for many of the railway hotels' interiors in the first two decades of the 20th century. She was responsible for the various interiors of the Banff Springs from 1905—when she and her husband lived in Banff—to the late 1920s.

The new tower included a dining room, a large rotunda that became the central lobby of the hotel (now the Rundle Lounge), and rooms for over 300 guests. Much of the new public floor space was done in imported red English tile, which was for decades the despair of the junior hotel bellboys, who were charged with keeping each individual tile outlined with a fresh coat of black paint. The meticulous construction of the building as a whole was not going to be diminished by inattention to the smallest detail of upkeep.

Today, in a nod to the past, a single row of the old Kate Reed red tiles can be seen beneath the grill railing that protects the top of the small stairwell connecting Mezzanine Levels One and Two, just west of the Rundle Lounge.

The completed centre tower, 1915.

Wicker furniture and hanging plants were hallmarks of Kate Reed's design.

HOTEL CHAMELEON

The rockwork held a surprise for the people who worked on the "new" hotel. It changed colour! As quarried, Rundlestone has a bluish-grey tinge that, with extended exposure to the sun, turns to a rich brown. It was with some incredulity, then, that early labourers returned to the hotel after a few years' absence to discover their blue castle was brown. Today's visitors can observe the difference between the two shades of rock by standing out front of the hotel's main entrance and looking up. The exterior walls of the entrance, which is a relatively recent addition to the hotel, are a cool, blue-grey. The walls of the original building, above the entrance, have the warm brown colour characteristics of the older hotel.

Looking across to the Banff Springs Hotel from Surprise Corner, 1920.

Princes and Politicians

"AS HAPPY AS GRIGS, WHATEVER A GRIG MAY BE."

Although Painter's sketches included two new wings as well as the centre tower—meaning, in effect, a completely new structure—his role in the construction ended with the tower. Upon the tower's completion, the CPR's upper echelon decided to ease back and see what could be accomplished with the new tower and the two older wings. It would be 14 years before the rest of Painter's plans, with major modifications by another architect, became a reality.

The intervening years were prosperous for the Banff Springs, and successive managements worked diligently to polish the hotel's already established reputation as one of the continent's great luxury resorts.

Over the years, the hotel had become more and more of a summer home for a number of its guests, and by 1914 many of the visitors were seasoned Banff veterans, with 10 or more years of "Springing" under their belts. The Duke and Duchess of Connaught became seasonal repeats when they returned in August 1914 for a two-week stay. Their entourage occupied 22 rooms of the new tower, and their servants occupied an additional 10.

"Banff and its surroundings have brought fame to the Province of Alberta because of the wonders of the Canadian Rockies, and the natural beauty of its scenery summer and winter. 'Conceit' is declared to be the only photoplay that has carried practically its entire action into that rugged country, bringing to the screen, in this way, scenery that will be a revelation to theatregoers who may have glimpsed the Canadian Rockies only in news reels or educationals."

– *Conceit* review, 1921

The duke had regrets about leaving Banff on his first visit in 1912, but he had even greater regrets about departing in 1914. Returning to Banff from a canoe trip on the Bow River one afternoon, he saw a line of scarlet-clad Mounties standing in rank along the riverbank. His guide, Jim Brewster, heard him mutter, "Ah, yes, I expected this," before he lapsed into profound silence. When the canoe reached shore, the Mounties presented the duke with Great Britain's declaration of war and told him a train was waiting at the railway station. Within a few hours, he was steaming east across the prairies, heading towards home and the Great War.

The following year, another high-profile guest had regrets about departing Banff, but for very different reasons. Carrying a light fishing rod and speaking at full volume, the Rough Rider president of the United States, Theodore Roosevelt, was in town and staying at the Springs. Banff, it appears, appealed to him.

I am DEE-LIGHTED with your town. Banff is the centre of all that is beautiful, and this part of the mountains is the Yellowstone Park of Canada. I regret exceedingly my time is so limited as nothing would give me greater pleasure than to spend several weeks catching your justly celebrated mountain trout.

The parade of princes, politicians, and patrons continued unimpeded throughout the decade. In 1920 the hotel expanded its celebrity horizons by entertaining the Hollywood cast of *Conceit*, which was the first of many movies with a full theatrical release to be filmed near Banff. The stars—Betty Hilburn, Maurice Costello, Hedda Hopper, and William Davidson—had ample opportunity to become familiar with Banff during their stay. The company travelled to Banff "for outdoor spring scenes," Hopper recalled in her memoir. "But on our arrival spring was muffled to the top of the trees in snow and ice. We settled down to wait for the thaw. For three months we waited. No one in the Selznick company had thought to check on the weather in Banff. We had a delightful time, though, skating and tobogganing, while we waited."

The movie and its leading lights helped spread the word about the Canadian Rockies, and glamorous names associated with the film world began to appear more frequently on the pages of the Banff Springs Register.

The hotel, in the meantime, if not growing its footprint, was busy with renovation and innovation. The east wing of the original

Lew Cody spent time at the hotel while filming The Valley of the Silent Men *in 1922. This scene was shot near what is now Tunnel Mountain Campground.*

A four-horse covered tally-ho loads in front of the lobby for sightseeing in the 1920s.

1888 building, which had served for many years as the dining room and kitchen, was torn down in 1915, and some 400 guest rooms were newly decorated for the start of the 1916 season. The summer of 1916 also introduced Japanese bellboys and waitresses. As well, a society press agent was hired to chronicle "the arrival and doings of all prominent society people" and to see that such arrivals and doings were duly noted by North America's media.

Other alterations occurred during the winter of 1916, when the hotel was allotted $140,000 for the construction of another new boiler room and laundry. Obviously not included in the alterations was an upgraded telephone service: the faults of the existing one caused one frustrated visitor to remark that one had as much chance of reaching the desired party "as winning the pot against a royal flush."

Another complaint levied against the hotel between 1914 and 1920 came not from the guests but other hotel owners in Banff. By virtue of owning the railway that ran through the town, the local railway station, and a large hotel, the CPR exercised a healthy power of persuasion over the town's potential visitors. Simply by advertising the CPR hotels on CPR trains and making sure the CPR carriage held the favoured platform position at the CPR station, the company ensured a capacity-level crowd for the Banff Springs Hotel.

The owners of the other hotels in town resented such lopsided practices, and in the summer of 1915 several of them arranged a meeting with two CPR officials to air their

The Banff Springs Hotel lobby, 1920.

grievances. The company officers listened to the charges and promised to allow literature about other Banff accommodation on the trains. But they remained adamant that the CPR hotel would retain all other "privileges of the platform."

The settlement temporarily soothed most tempers, but in August 1915 the local newspaper ran an editorial that brought the issue back to a head. While stating that the paper had no particular desire to roast the CPR, the editorial presented evidence that someone connected to the CPR in the east was advising railway passengers that the Banff Springs Hotel was the only hotel in Banff, and that if travellers couldn't get a reservation at the Springs they'd be wise to travel on without stopping. That such advice was being dispersed was "vouched for by residents of unimpeachable integrity," but whether it was being dispersed maliciously or merely through misinformation is an open question.

Another editorial in the same paper provided an interesting insight into the attack on the hotel. The 1915 season was supposed to be a banner year for Banff, but it fell far short of predictions. The editorial suggested the CPR's "dog-in-the-manger" attitude was responsible for the situation. By failing to provide sufficient advertising about Rocky

Mountains Park and the availability of good, plentiful accommodation in Banff, the CPR and Dominion government had cost the town much potential business from tourists returning to their homes in the east from the 1915 Panama-Pacific International Exposition in San Francisco. The editorial speculated that exposition attendees were choosing southern routes through other, better-advertised areas such as the Grand Canyon. The whole problem, in hindsight, appears to have centred around the search for a scapegoat for a less than terrific season.

Another controversial issue of the era – one that would soon change forever the complexion of the town, tourism, and the park – was the introduction of automobiles

BANFF REVISITED

Born in London, England, in 1857, Morley Roberts had travelled the world by the time he passed through Banff in 1884 on his way west to find work with the CPR. By the time Roberts returned to Banff in 1925, he was an accomplished writer, with many short stories and books to his credit. His second visit was the basis of a new book, *On the Old Trail: Through British Columbia After Forty Years*, published in 1927, in which he found the Banff Springs Hotel beyond credulity:

Morley Roberts during his Western travels.

The truth is that I could not take beautiful Banff seriously. I dreamed it, and like so many dreams it was at once absurd and beautiful. On a pine-covered bank or bluff above the crystal foam of the Bow I came to a gigantic castle. It had no business being there, for when I was thereabouts so long ago no one could have thought of it. It was full of the most curious looking people who seemed very busy about nothing at all but were as happy as grigs, whatever a grig may be. They wore all kinds of odd costumes. Some women, so greatly determined on being noticed as to defy ridicule flaunted about in long shining boots and scarlet jackets and jockey caps, while others wore clothes "made in America" in the back woods, which looked as if they had been cut out with an axe. The dream castle was full of such people who talked all at once and I saw in a moment that they were not real. I, or someone else, had imagined them. If any of us workers of the old days had seen their likes we should have thought we had delirium tremens at the least.

An aerial view of the hotel in the mid-1920s.

to the town and park. Following the 1903 request of a Calgary auto-owner to ship his car to Banff via rail and then drive it around town, the park administrators, notably supported by the head of the CPR hotel department, argued successfully for an order-in-council prohibiting automobile use on park roads.

Motoring enthusiasts, however, were not to be denied. In August, 1909, Norman Lougheed of Calgary became the first person to drive from Calgary to Banff in an epic eight-and-a-half hour journey along the partially completed Calgary-Banff Coach Road. Triumphantly reaching Banff, he was immediately arrested and charged.

As it turned out, however, his arrest was not in vain. Two years later, as Banff historian Ted Hart recounts: ". . . a cavalcade of Calgary Automobile Club members arrived in town and drove their 'buzz wagons' everywhere, including across the Spray bridge and onto the Loop to attend the official opening ceremonies of the Banff Springs Golf Course."

By 1918, the resistance had crumbled and a new order-in-council was passed that allowed motorists to drive into Banff, with the proviso, as Hart explains, that automobile owners "register with the superintendent or the police, pay a fee, and drive directly by way of Banff and Spray avenues to their place of accommodation." Also, according to the order, they had to "manage and control such motor vehicle in such manner as to exercise every reasonable precaution to prevent the frightening of any . . . horses. . . ."

One favourite stopping place was the confluence of the Banff and Spray Rivers, directly below the Banff Springs. Both the hotel and the park officials, concerned by the increasing congregation of automobiles – the owners of which had begun to camp by the Bow Falls – found a solution in creating the park's first campground on the far side of the Spray River.

Except for the noise of the buzz wagons and a few more people sharing the view of the Bow Falls, visitors at the hotel were largely unaffected by such downtown matters. Outside the castle walls, guests were free to enjoy their wilderness activities, and inside they remained unencumbered in their pursuit of social superiority. For the British, the rankings game was often played at the expense of their ever-suffering American counterparts. According to the local paper dated August 12, 1922:

"A newly rich American, a class which is flooding the country just now, approached an English gentleman in the Banff Springs Hotel recently with the query: 'Say, where is the lavatory?' The Englishman coolly looked his questioner over and replied: 'Go down that corridor and turn to the right where you will see a door with the sign Gentlemen on it, but don't let that deter you, old top."

Beyond the occasional unexpected peculiarity, such as the non-fatal shooting of a guest in 1920 and an equally intriguing charge of "bigamy" levied against two staff members in 1922, the good life swirled on, and the Banff Springs settled in for a lively decade of gilded extravagance.

Brewster touring cars on Vermilion Lakes Road in the 1920s.

Demolition of the original south wing, 1927.

Out of the Fire

"IT WAS ONE OF THE MOST BEAUTIFULLY AND CAREFULLY FINISHED BUILDINGS ON THE CONTINENT, AND NO EXPENSE HAD BEEN SPARED TO MAKE IT SO."

By 1925, the time had come to complete the plans drawn up in 1911. As early as the fall of 1921, the CPR had authorized nearly $2 million for the destruction of the old wooden wings of the hotel and their replacement by rock-faced, fireproof structures. The record season of 1922, which saw 400 to 500 guests registered daily throughout July and August (a grand seasonal tally of some 52,000 visitors), provided a compelling rationale for further expansion.

The new wings would be built over the course of two years—one erected during the winter of 1926–27, and the other the following winter. First, though, it was necessary to build a separate annex to accommodate the regular hotel guests while the wings were being replaced. Thus, at the close

On April 6, 1926, the hotel's north wing was destroyed by fire.

of the 1925 season, a four-storey, 100-room building was constructed adjacent to the south wing. With a grey cement-finished exterior and decorative allusions to the Tudor style, it broke with the hotel's château motif. A short time later, a second building was constructed. (Once the new wings were finished and the guests back in the hotel proper, the two outlying buildings became staff accommodation. Then known as the Lower and Upper Annex, both are now part of what is called the Gatehouse.)

The work on the Lower Annex was completed towards the end of March 1926, which proved to be none too soon. On April 6, at 11 a.m., the hotel's assistant manager, Reginald Coysh, and a CPR publicity agent, Buffalo Child Long Lance, noticed smoke curling skyward from the hotel's north wing. Coysh filed a fire report immediately, and within an hour over 500 men were at the hotel fighting an enormous blaze. The old wooden wing burned brightly and rapidly, and by 2 p.m. the last of the original 1888 hotel was a pile of smouldering debris. Far from being able to save the wing, the firefighters, including some who raced in from Calgary, had to be content with rescuing as much furniture as possible and trying to limit the damage to the centre tower.

While the tower shielded the south wing from harm, the tower itself sustained grievous

The north wing, the last section of the original hotel, lies as a smouldering ruin.

injury when a major explosion in the basement blew out many of its windows and fittings. Further, the fire managed to spread from the old wing into the tower and gut the gracious 13-year-old dining room. Flames also struck the tower's north and west faces. The smoke-stained surfaces can still be seen today on the walls rising above the Garden Terrace.

The cause of the fire was attributed to labourers doing some preseason, preconstruction blasting around the north wing's base. They had built a fire close to the old wing and the flames made their way unnoticed to the main building.

Rumours at the time theorized that the fire had been set intentionally under orders from CPR officials. No evidence supports the claim, though. Any such fire would be sure to delay the opening of the hotel and greatly reduce its capacity during what promised to be a highly lucrative summer. Also, the idea that any hotel would risk the adverse publicity of a fire is simply bad thinking.

That said, a more fortuitous time for a fire would only have been during the fall of the same year. As it was, the fire occurred before the start of the tourist season—well before the arrival of any guests. As well, the wing was scheduled to be torn down at the end of the season, and financing and designs for its replacement were already in place.

Following the fire, the CPR acted with a speed and precision that would have befitted old Van Horne. Sir Edward Beatty, president of the CPR from 1918 to 1943, was on the scene within a matter of days, and it was decided that construction on the new wing would begin immediately. A generous budget of $2 million was allocated for the construction and for the restoration of the centre tower. Work was well underway when the hotel belatedly opened its doors on July 1, 1926.

The man in charge of designing the new wings was John W. Orrock, a CPR engineer whose ideas were compatible with Painter's. Using the general style of the old wooden wings (to which Painter also paid homage in his 1911 sketches for a new hotel), Orrock inked the final additions, making both the north and south wings much larger than those Painter had planned and angling the towers of the wings gracefully away from the river. He enlarged the centre wing (the lower section of the centre tower) and modified its roofline, which enabled him to tie the earlier structure solidly to the new wings.

The north wing was the first to be replaced, and the project proceeded rapidly, albeit not so smoothly as might have been wished. In October 1926, a worker was killed and two others seriously injured when a lift derrick collapsed and a steel beam weighing some 2,500 pounds dropped a full three storeys onto the men working below. In February the following year, another man was badly injured as he looked down an elevator shaft and yelled at someone on the lower floor to send up some tile. His timing was off (or perhaps his powers of observation) and the lift came down on his head. Construction humour allowed that Bill lost his head in the excitement of getting the tile laid. In truth, his head remained attached to his body and he survived to work another day. The elevator, though, was not to be robbed of its grisly prize, and in May it claimed the life of a worker who was greasing it, an accident held to be the unfortunate fellow's own fault.

The north wing was constructed with the same methodology used in building the centre tower 14 years earlier. A steel frame was erected, and then, around the steel, a massive plank cocoon that provided shelter for the labourers who continued with the concrete and rock work throughout the winter. In the spring of 1927, less than a year after the

A plank cocoon allowed construction to continue on the north wing through the winter of 1926-27.

great fire, the cocoon fell away and a new limestone wing stretched towards the distant peak of Cascade Mountain.

While the new north wing rose from the ashes of the old efficiently and quickly, the south wing went up even faster. With construction beginning in September 1927, it took just seven months—until April 1928—for the south wing to emerge from its cocoon. If that feat were not sufficiently impressive, the crew also found time to extend and rebuild both the inner and outer swimming pools. Of note, the new inner pool was an enclosed one, a change that required substituting fresh water for the previous pool's sulphur waters. An interior sulphur pool would have led to a hotel permeated by the smell of rotten eggs, a state of affairs that would have dampened even the most fervent "Springers'" enthusiasm for staying there.

The swift pace of the work ensured the hotel would be ready for the start of the 1928 season. As spring yielded to summer, people throughout North America and Europe learned that for the second time in 15 years, a "new" Banff Springs Hotel was awaiting their arrival. An inspection team from the CPR, headed by none other than Sir Edward Beatty himself, was on hand for the opening ceremonies on May 15, 1928.

As it turned out, Sir Edward and his crew were none too early for their inspection tour. As remembered by one witness, whenever Beatty turned his back, a carpenter or mason would emerge from the shadows to put a quick final touch on some not-quite-finished component of the hotel. Such activities were discreetly undertaken and kept as far as possible from Sir Edward, who had been promised the hotel would be finished by his arrival. Much to the credit of the workmen and those coordinating their efforts, Beatty never did learn of their secretive tapping and polishing.

Nor did he learn that his company's hotel construction had also supported the parallel construction of two private Banff residences. It seems that one of the men carting construction supplies from the railway station to the hotel was chronically unable to keep a full load on his wagon. Part of each shipment slipped off at a particular spot along the route, and he never managed to get it all back on. Miraculously, the lost materials subsequently arose from the side of the dust road in the form of two modest single-family dwellings.

What Beatty did learn, however, was that highly polished oak floors can be slippery. Recovering his balance and his dignity after a near tumble in the Alhambra Dining Room (which had originally been planned as a ballroom), he ordered that the entire floor,

Looking down on the construction of the south wing from Sulphur Mountain in 1927.

so painstakingly and expensively finished, be carpeted immediately.

More to his liking was the décor of the new Vice Regal Suite, the grandest of the 32 suites the hotel could boast about. A shining example of medieval opulence, the suite, with its three sitting rooms and 10 bedrooms, was designed and decorated to ensure the Banff Springs would continue to look after royal-calibre visitors in a fashion befitting their status.

SWEET SUITE

The sitting area of the Vice Regal Suite in the 1920s.

For six decades, the Vice Regal Suite served as the Banff Springs' preeminent retreat for royalty, heads of state, celebrities, and other notables. Occupying the sixth floor of the south wing, it was a sumptuous collection of the best the hotel had to offer. It included its own reception foyer, a dining room, three sitting rooms, and 10 bedrooms, as well as vaulted ceilings, heavy oak trim and furniture, reproductions of old paintings, tapestries, richly coloured Persian rugs, and, of course, beautiful views over the Spray River to Mount Rundle. Lest there be any question as to the loyalties of the suite's creators, the foyer sported a portrait of Henry VIII and, at either end, the British royal coat of arms.

The suite definitely lived up to its name, accommodating, among many others, King George VI and Queen Elizabeth I, Prince Philip, Lord Mountbatten, Indian prime minister Indira Gandhi, Prince Rainier of Monaco, and Canadian prime ministers Lester Pearson and Pierre Trudeau. In what was perhaps a sign of changing times, Alberta's premier Peter Lougheed stayed in the suite on a visit to Banff in the late 1960s but thereafter requested other rooms, saying he wasn't enamoured with the old-fashioned style of the Vice Regal and preferred a more modern suite.

Today, the suite has a new name, new décor, and a new configuration that centres on a single two-bedroom deluxe suite. From that core structure, however, the arrangement can be expanded as required via a private foyer that connects to other bedrooms and yet more suites. In honour of the art that graces the suite—works of the great wildlife painter Carl Rungius—the rooms are known as the Gallery Suite.

The hotel's front entrance in the 1920s.

Indeed, Beatty found the entire hotel much to his liking. If the original 1888 hotel had been a place of refined elegance, the "new" hotel was one of haughty grandeur—one of the most beautifully and carefully finished buildings on the continent, and no expense had been spared to make it so.

Though obviously influenced by Scottish and French architecture and exhibiting the massive walls and steep roofs Bruce Price thought essential for northern architecture, the 1928 hotel was ultimately its own building. It presented a distinctive, homogenous appearance in spite of all its different influences.

The hotel's interior elements, on the other hand, were as heterogeneous as its exterior elements were homogeneous. While probably not an intended outcome, the contrasting motifs throughout the hotel reflected the reality of many European castles—in which successive owners had altered their properties in piecemeal fashion to fit their own tastes, budgets, and the changing styles of the times. Many of the diverse elements of the 1928 hotel are still present today, and most guests

The Alhambra Dining Room in the late 1920s (above) was the hotel's most formal restaurant. In the same vicinity of the property, Mount Stephen Hall, pictured below in the 1920s, remains one of the hotel's grandest public spaces.

No expense was spared when it came to decorating the Conservatory.

agree that the variety adds a visual energy that would otherwise be lacking.

Equally as interesting as the different styles is the lavish and detailed presentation of those styles. In keeping with hotel tradition, the CPR spared no expense when it came to decorating the 1928 hotel. For example, to enhance the Spanish motif of the Alhambra Room, which served as the hotel's formal dining room until 1972, the company spent $30,000 to have replicas made of the doors of the Alhambra palace in Granada, Spain. Wrought of brass in Montreal, each door weighs a full ton. Bedford lime flagstones were imported from Indiana for the floor of Mount Stephen Hall, and for certain decorative work the company brought in Tyndall limestone—famous for being laced with 450-million-year-old fossils—from Garson, Manitoba. No less impressive, to properly frame the "million dollar view" from the Riverview Lounge, the company commissioned eight arched windows from Czechoslovakia. Weighing 300 pounds each, the single pane windows required custom-fitted boxcars for transport from Europe.

Remarkably, the full set of Riverview windows stayed intact until 1988, when an irate wife

FOSSIL HUNTING

One of the fossils on the lower stairs of the Rundle Lounge.

The mottled Tyndall Stone featured in some of the Banff Springs' floors, stairways, windowsills, and fireplaces constitutes a particularly unusual feature of the hotel. Formed in ancient seabeds, the predominant cream-coloured part of the stone is limestone, while the twisting mottled parts are dolomite. The dolomite patterns were created when an unidentified species of sea creature burrowed into the limestone. However, the stone is primarily noted for its ancient marine fossils, including corals, brachiopods, gastropods, cephalopods, snails, nautiloids, and trilobites, many as old as 450 million years. In places where the rock has been worn, such as on the circular stairway near the Alhambra Room, the Tyndall Stone takes on a special lustre and the fossils stand out in high relief. As a guest listening to a concert in Mount Stephen Hall discovered, "A strange emotion comes over one who traces with his finger a fossilized trilobite on a windowsill while listening to the music of a modern orchestra."

A good place to admire the fossils is in the lower Rundle Lounge, on the third stair from the bottom of the stairway rising to Mezzanine Level 2. Stone containing the most prominent fossils was placed on the lower stairs, allowing those who stop to admire them to do so from the safety of floor level. The largest fossil in the hotel, a trilobite some 14 inches long, is in the floor behind the desk in the VIP lounge adjoining the Rundle Lounge.

The Oak Room in the 1920s.

threw a chair at her husband one night. The husband ducked, and the chair went through one of the famous windows. One can only speculate as to how angry the woman must have been to throw a chair in such a public space—and how embarrassed she much have been once she realized what she had done.

The company, of course, was determined to have workmanship commensurate with the quality of the imported materials, and officials demanded that the greatest care be exhibited in executing the smallest decorative details. The oak wainscoting, the linenfold (wood or stone carved to depict folded linen), the animal carvings, the delicate plasterwork (such as that gracing the mushroom ceiling of the circular stairway near the Alhambra Room), the highly polished terrazzo floors, the Tiffany light fixtures, the intricate stained glass and great carved oak beams of Mount Stephen Hall, and the numerous and varied angels, gargoyles, and indigenous people that peer at unsuspecting guests from dark corners exhibit a patience and devotion to fine craftsmanship that has all but disappeared in the modern era. As one proud staff member pointed out, even the radiator covers are minor masterpieces.

Many of the furnishings of the "new" hotel remain on display today, and are a major factor in creating the rich, textured baronial atmosphere of the hotel's great halls. Many of the 1928 hotel's tapestries, prints, rugs, and furniture pieces were selected by Michael Delahanty, a former manager of the hotel, and Kate Treleaven, a personal secretary to Sir Edward Beatty. The Leonardo Society of Montreal helped with the reproduction selection.

The furniture of the 1928 hotel, representing a wide span of styles and periods, was

The impressive brass doors leading to the Alhambra Room are an impressive feature to this day.

made by the Montreal firm Castle & Son Manufacturing, and all pieces are exact reproductions of original period furniture. In fact, the reproductions are so precise that the plane marks on the original surfaces are rendered in them. The pieces chosen for reproduction were discovered in various European castles, manors, monasteries, and palaces, and a number of the reproductions were reputedly sourced from the castles of Banffshire in Scotland.

Many of the prints that grace the walls of the hotel are Gothic and Renaissance in origin and are certainly in keeping with the general mood of the great halls. It is interesting to note, though, that during the 1930s, some of the prints in the private rooms proved too sombre for the guests. The housekeepers quickly learned which were least acceptable as they would routinely find them taken down and turned towards the wall.

Two other paintings, more contemporary and certainly less gloomy, are interesting for their links to the CPR. One of them, depicting an Ontario forest, hangs at the north end of the Spanish Walk—the upper, open gallery that traces the west wall of Mount Stephen Hall and connects the elevator lobby on Mezzanine Level 2 with the Alhambra Room. The artist was none other than Van Horne, who painted the piece in 1903 and then whimsically signed his name backwards in the lower right-hand corner, reputedly in reference to the original hotel's being built the wrong way around.

The other painting, measuring over six square metres (65 square feet), hangs at the top of the Rundle Lounge's grand stairway. While the painting's topic—a lumberman on the Miramichi River in New Brunswick felling trees for use as masts for the British navy—seemingly has little to do with a hotel in Banff, the pioneer feller is William Davidson, an early European settler who grew up in Moray, near Banffshire in Scotland. Further, the painting is by Cyrus Cuneo (1879–1916), one of the artists involved in the CPR's early arts-promotion program.

The hotel prides itself on its wide selection of furniture pieces, oriental rugs, tapestries, and excellent prints, and it maintains a large workshop with staff to keep the pieces in good repair. At one time the hotel kept a "furniture blueprint" of all the building's public spaces—plans that showed exactly where each piece of furniture, mirror, print, tapestry, and rug was to be placed and kept.

All in all, the 1928 hotel exhibited a rich profusion of different styles, furnishings, and objets d'art. By virtue of their craftsmanship and the good taste that informed their acquisition, they collectively created a grand baronial atmosphere: a scene set beautifully for what many considered the hotel's most glamorous era.

Looking out to the Bow Valley from the Riverview Lounge in the 1920s.

Tour buses passing by the Banff Springs Hotel.

A Brief but Golden Moment

"WHO ARE THEY, THESE BUTTERFLY LADIES IN THEIR PARIS GOWNS?"

In the Banff Springs Hotel's long and glittering history, one era, stretching from the completion of the 1928 hotel to the outbreak of World War II, is particularly dazzling. During the late 1920s and the 1930s, the hotel came tantalizingly close to fulfilling all of the fantasies one might have about life at a luxury hotel.

Not that anything much had changed, at least at first glimpse, from the earlier days. The hotel's traditions remained unchanged, princes and politicians still frequented the halls, money moved easily from one manicured hand to another, and comments concerning the hotel carried the same tenor in 1937 as in 1897. For example, in 1909, a prominent New York journalist claimed the following:

Between New York and Shanghai . . . there is no spot more cosmopolitan than the rotunda of the C.P. Hotel at Banff . . . The women in this group of people in the rotunda of the hotel are dressed as attractively as any women in any hotel in the world, and when the orchestra plays and the people move about talking to each other I could imagine myself in Buenos Aires, in Bombay, in Melbourne, in Malta, in Cape Town or in any other city in which the currents of the world come together.

And 28 years later, in 1937, a London writer exclaimed:

Of one or two places in the world it has been said that if we would but bide there a while we would see all our friends, in due course, pass by. Of such and such a chair at the Café de la Paix in Paris that has been said, and of the Strand Corner, in London, by Charing Cross. To the number of these places I would add the Banff Springs Hotel. Sit in the portico there, and in due time all your old friendships will be renewed.

But there was a difference between the pre-World War I era, characterized by the brisk and measured step of propriety, and the *entre deux guerres* era, perhaps best described by the phrase "cultured ease." The Great War dealt a crushing blow to Europe's moneyed classes, who, with high Victorian idealism, considered themselves responsible for, and in control of, the ebb and flow of the world's fortunes. The weight of social responsibility manifested, in part, as personal propriety—one had to wear the accountabilities of one's money in an exemplary fashion. The war was as ugly as war can be, and the dark smoke hanging over the Marne, Vimy Ridge, and Ypres destroyed the elite's self-congratulatory esteem. By the November armistice of 1918, little was left of the previous social tradition.

The world's wealthy, socially ranked families (from which the Banff Springs drew much of its clientele) started to view themselves and their riches in a new light, and they began to engineer an escape from the responsibilities thought to be implicit in wealth. The whale-boned Gibson Girl of the 1900s gave way to the casual flapper of the 1920s and the vamp of the 1930s. The collar was being loosened.

In time, the Great Depression's hard realities added their own curl to the changing narrative. Sudden uncertainty about the future forced many to reevaluate their thoughts about the present, and their conclusion was that they had better live as fully as possible, and do it today.

If the Banff Springs had been "sumptuous" at the turn of the 20th century, it was, by 1930, "truly extravagant." It was against this setting that many of the most interesting, amusing, and entertaining events in the hotel's history occurred. Awash with the amenities that attend a moneyed upbringing, the hotel practically vibrated with the quirks and idiosyncrasies that affluence can afford.

It was a time when people would arrive at the hotel with letters of credit worth $50,000, a sum earmarked specifically for a 60-to-90-day stay in Banff. "The men," reported one banker guest, "would fish and play golf, and the women would change their clothes." There was a staff of 10 porters who did nothing but ferry luggage from the station to the hotel and back, and a special elevator had to be installed to handle the huge steamer trunks that seemed to be an indispensable part of the whole experience.

Waitresses filling orders, 1920s.

The outdoor swimming pool at the Banff Springs Hotel was a popular hangout for hotel guests in the 1920s.

It was also a time when the old veneer of highbrow snobbishness was stretched dangerously thin. While many of the old-time seasonals undoubtedly preferred the more stolid propriety of the prewar period, a new era was afoot, bringing with it the shrieks of the young New York debutante who, having declared her boredom with life, found herself airborne in the direction of the swimming pool, $300 gown and all. In the same vein, it was taken as a matter of course that each Saturday night someone would squirm into the suit of armour that used to stand at the bottom of the staircase near the ballroom. By midsummer, even the newest staff would be habituated to the sound of an errant knight in his cups ricocheting down the dimly lit corridors.

Murray Adaskin, violinist for the Toronto Trio (and later one of Canada's foremost composers), gained a certain "highbrow/lowbrow" perspective the first night the trio performed at the hotel. Their task was to play for the dinner hour, and then, a bit later, present an hour-long concert in Mount Stephen Hall. As the dinner hour approached, Adaskin was told the trio was to play in the dining room's foyer, not the dining room itself, and that the trio's volume was to be more *piano* than *forte*. Although taken aback, the trio accepted the decree and played a subdued set of pieces throughout the dinner hour. It wasn't until the hotel manager and his wife emerged from the dining room that the musicians came to understand their directive. Approaching the young violinist,

The Toronto Trio (from left to right, Murray Adaskin, Louis Crerar, and Cornelius Ysselstyn) played 11 seasons at the hotel from 1930 to 1941.

the manager smiled and then whispered in his ear: "Just fine, Murray—didn't bother a soul!"

But if the manager wasn't able to appreciate fully the trio's talents, there were many who could. The Mount Stephen Hall concerts, presented six nights a week (on the seventh night local naturalist and author Dan McCowan gave a nature talk), were always well received by a discriminating and knowledgeable audience. Many members of the New York and Boston fine arts elite spent their summers at the hotel, and for more than one season Adaskin's programs were vetted and edited by a prominent patron of the Boston Symphony.

> *"A haven of gracious living in a setting of breath-taking beauty, where visitors from all over the world return year after year; for, once visited, Banff Springs calls again."*
>
> – *Castle in the Air*, CPR brochure, 1935

The arts actually played a vital role in creating and maintaining the hotel's image. Under the auspices of John Murray Gibbon, the CPR's general publicity agent, the Light Opera Company of Alfred Heather presented two operas a week throughout the summer seasons of 1930–32. Staged in the Cascade Ballroom, the operas featured many of the well-known singers of the day, including Randolph Crowe, Enid Gray, Frances James, and Allan Burt.

Gibbon—whose energies and interests seem to have matched those of Van Horne himself—also made full use of Van Horne's early marketing strategy of inviting well-known artists to participate in promotional railway junkets. The artists were given the opportunity to sketch, paint, and photograph the dramatic Western landscape, and the CPR could use the resulting images to promote what it billed as the "Canadian Pacific Rockies." In 1884, even before the railway was finished, Van Horne offered famed photographer William Notman an official CPR railway car with an adjoining darkroom car to capture "views" of the railway construction and the mountains as far as the end of the line. No sooner was Notman back in Montreal than Van Horne was busy selecting the best of an impressive collection of photographs for use in a brochure intended "to attract English Tourists [to Banff] before spring opens."

Under Gibbon's guidance, such artistic luminaries as Carl Rungius and Walter J. Phillips were invited to visit the Banff Springs and use it as a base for painting forays into the surrounding mountains. The plan worked well, although there was at least one instance when the arrangement backfired. In 1931, Rungius curtly dismissed from his presence a young man whom he took to be one of the Japanese bellboys. Carl was making final preparations for a show of four local artists—Rungius, Charlie Beil, Nicholas de Grandmaison, and Peter Whyte—and he was simply not to be distracted by superfluous requests from hotel staff. Only later did Rungius learn the "bellboy" had been an emissary from the Queen of Siam, who was seeking a special showing. Snubbed, the queen never did attend the show, and the artists missed out on what could have been a financially rewarding and reputation-enhancing connection.

Another artist, although best known for his endeavours in other arenas of life, visited the hotel in late August 1929. Winston Churchill, then 54 years old and taking a brief break from politics, was touring the United States and Canada with his son, brother, and nephew. Aside from touring the area, soaking in the hot springs, and enjoying a trail ride, Churchill tested his painting talents against the grandeur and challenging light of the surrounding mountains. As a former housekeeper recalls, Churchill clambered through the manager's office window to access a small balcony, from which he painted the view of the valley. The smell of his cigars wafted back through the executive offices. Churchill wrote to his wife about his visit, declaring the Banff Springs "a magnificent hotel with every comfort."

Tennis whites and dresses were de rigueur for the Banff Springs courts in the 1920s and '30s.

As important as the arts were, they were merely a sideshow, a rich embellishment, to the hotel's main draw: the mountains. Hikers fanned out across an expanding system of trails constructed by a combination of CPR and government money, and horseback trips to nearby scenic attractions were more in demand than ever. A riding club, the Order of the Trail Riders of the Canadian Rockies, was organized in the early 1920s, and by 1930 the CPR was touting a number of overnight backcountry cabins for use on extended rides. Mountain climbing, fishing, and canoeing remained popular activities, and, weather permitting, the golf course and tennis courts were fully booked day after day.

THE RAILWAY SCHOOL

Just as the design of the CPR hotels gave birth to Canada's first national school of architecture, the company's use of visual art to promote itself played a vital role in the creation of Canada's first national school of art.

At the time that Canada's architects were wrestling with the question of a national style, Canadian artists were searching for a national focus. British and European artists of the day were committed to exploring the "sublime in nature," a trend that influenced Canadian art as well. Canada, after all, had no end of untrammelled landscapes with distinctly northern characteristics, and some of the most highly regarded artists in the country had built reputations on their ability to portray them.

According to historian Ted Hart, the determination that nature was an appropriate subject for art overlapped Canada's "awakening spirit of nationalism and interest in the northwest spawned by the building of the transcontinental line."

Conveniently, it also overlapped Van Horne's zeal for visual advertising. Drawing inspiration from the US railways, Van Horne decided to publish high-quality tourist brochures and booklets incorporating his own text and the best available mountain illustrations. Since few good illustrations of the Canadian Rockies existed, he had to initiate a program to create some. His strategy was to give free rail passes to the foremost landscape artists with the stipulation that they paint the mountains "to the exclusion of anything else." In return, the CPR would have first pick of the resulting art.

Early beneficiaries of the much-coveted CPR passes were Lucius O'Brien, John Arthur Fraser, Thomas Mower Martin, and Frederic Marlett Bell-Smith. Their paintings, sketches, and watercolours came to symbolize Canadian art in the 19th century, and the "railway school of art" became Canada's first "national" school of art. Other artists associated with the program in later decades included the likes of Belmore Browne, Nicholas de Grandmaison, A. C. Leighton, Walter Phillips, and Carl Rungius.

The program continued for decades, and one of the many paintings it produced—a rendering of Mount Hurd by Frederic Marlett Bell-Smith—was printed as a commemorative stamp in 1928.

In 2013, after a hiatus of many years, a modified Artist in Residence program was reintroduced in a partnership between Fairmont Hotels and Mountain Galleries, which operates retail art outlets in several Fairmont properties. During the summer months, a

Two other activities sponsored by the hotel reached special prominence during the "golden era." One was Banff Indian Days, an institution already close to 40 years old by 1930. One year Helen Keller, the famous American deaf-blind author, activist, and lecturer, visited the Banff Springs during the midsummer festival and was made an honorary princess by the Stoney Nakoda people.

The other happening was the Banff Highland Gathering and Scottish Music Festival. Launched by John Murray Gibbon in 1927 as part of his CPR arts programming, the Gathering aligned well with Banff's purported

variety of well-known Canadian artists enjoys a week's stay at the Banff Springs Hotel, Jasper Park Lodge, or the Château Whistler, where they give painting demonstrations, converse with guests, and display their work in studios provided by Mountain Galleries.

Frederic Marlett Bell-Smith painted Morning, Lake Louise *in 1899.*

Scottish connections and soon achieved national recognition. Featuring Highland dancing and dress, regimental piping, and Caledonian athletics, the festival has a special flavour, as captured in the 1931 program notes:

When the Highland Gathering [came] to Banff, the Scots of Western Canada rolled up in their thousands to attend and take part, the pipes skirled, the dancers danced, and kilts swung and there was a brave array of tartans in the forest

TRAIL RIDERS AND HIKERS OF THE CANADIAN ROCKIES

In 1923, an eclectic group of outdoor enthusiasts decided to organize a horseback ride to promote the Canadian Rockies. Partly for personal reasons, partly for Banff Springs Hotel promotion, CPR publicist John Murray Gibbon agreed to sponsor what was to become a popular event via the Order of the Trail Riders of the Canadian Rockies. The committee behind the inaugural 1924 ride included such celebrities as Dr. Charles D. Walcott, secretary of the Smithsonian Institute; William T. Hornaday, director of the New York Zoological Society; and noted wildlife artist Carl Rungius. Also included were Banff locals Mary Schäffer, Jim and Bill Brewster, and Jimmy Simpson.

The inaugural Skyline Hikers of the Canadian Rockies outing was guided to Sentinel Pass, above Moraine Lake.

The first gathering was held in the Yoho Valley. The 207 riders slept in tepees, enjoyed hearty camp cooking, and listened to music played on a piano that was carried into camp on horseback. Riders were awarded pins based on the mileage ridden, and it is a testament to the members' equestrian passion that 97 of them had received their 2,500-mile pin by 1927.

Understanding that not everyone was comfortable on horseback, Gibbon went on to establish the Skyline Hikers of the Canadian Rockies. Mandated in 1933 to encourage hiking on Rocky Mountain trails, preserve national parks, and promote interest in flora and fauna, the Skyline Hikers followed the Trail Riders' winning formula of comfortable base camps, good food, and rousing campfire sing-alongs.

The CPR sponsored the sister organizations until 1961, when it gave notice that owing to changing times and demographics it could no longer carry their costs. Both groups quickly reorganized as nonprofit organizations, and the CPR generously sold its entire collection of camping paraphernalia to the organizers for $1.00. Both groups continue to flourish, although restrictions by Parks Canada mean they now have to vary trips in the parks with trips in other wilderness areas.

On August 1, 1928, local outfitter Tom Wilson hit the ceremonial first shot on the new Stanley Thompson-designed golf course.

clearing under the serrated peaks of these grim, gray Rockies.

Although the Highland Gathering was unable to sustain itself for more than a decade, most of the guests and townspeople who participated remembered it with a special fondness. Its demise was uncharitably attributed by some to the frugal nature of the Scots. It was said that while they enjoyed the festivities at the Banff Springs, they preferred to save their pennies by taking lodging at the downtown hotels.

While Banff Indian Days and the Highland Gathering were very different events, they did hold one thing in common—CPR promotion and lots of CPR money. Indeed, the CPR's open-purse policy of the late 1920s and the 1930s supported a propensity for extravagance that could equal or best that of its most extravagant guests.

The evolution of the golf course is a good example of the lengths to which the hotel could, and would, go to cater to its guests. A new course, redesigned and expanded from

Banff Indian Days, 1926.

the original layout to 18 holes, opened to public fanfare in 1924—and was then almost immediately taken back to the CPR drawing board in pursuit of something even better.

Preeminent course architect Stanley Thompson—a flamboyant character noted for his natty attire, love of whisky, and colourful stories—was hired to design yet another layout to replace the existing course. Unveiled in 1928, the new Banff Springs Golf Course was the most expensive ever built, having cost over half a million dollars. Topsoil for the fairways was imported from the prairies and sand for the generous bunkers was introduced from British Columbia. A special grass imported from the south proved to be popular not only with golfers but also with local elk. A solid Tudor-style stone clubhouse, with a dining room, patio, locker rooms, and pro shop, was constructed next to the first tee.

At 6,625 yards from the back markers, with a par of 73, the course was considered to be one of the toughest on the continent—and one of the most beautiful. Thompson's new layout incorporated some of the previous holes but also included some stunning new ones. "Devil's Cauldron," for example, playing across a small glacial lake nestled below the sheer face of Mount Rundle, is still one of the most famously scenic holes in the world of golf. The ceremonial opening shot was hit on August 1, 1928, by the pioneering outfitter Tom Wilson.

The golf course epitomized the hotel's devotion to continual improvement. When management decided that the horse trail near the hotel was too dusty, 400 tons of oak bark were imported from Ontario for a three-metre (six-foot) wide, six-kilometre (four-mile) long dustless trail dubbed "Rotten Row" in honour of London's famous equestrian grounds.

The hotel was equally attentive to the needs of its individual guests. For instance, when

SHE CLIMBS TO CONQUER

One visitor in the early 1930s who made particularly good use of her time was a 24-year-old New Yorker named Georgia Engelhard. The niece of artist Georgia O'Keefe and photographer Arthur Stieglitz, Engelhard fell in love with the Canadian Rockies when her parents introduced her to them in 1926.

In 1931, already an accomplished mountaineer and a photographer, she returned to star in a documentary produced by the National Parks of Canada. Entitled *She Climbs to Conquer,* the film made demands of Engelhard that few other actors could have handled. In just nine days, she had to climb Mount Victoria—the famous peak rising from the back of Lake Louise—no fewer than seven times.

Georgia Engelhard

In 1932, using the Banff Springs Hotel and the Château Lake Louise as her base, Engelhard set a single-season climbing record by scaling 38 separate mountains, including Mount Assiniboine (3,618 metres/11,870 feet), between her arrival on May 25 and her departure on October 15.

a Doctor Fowler from New York demanded fresh goat's milk at mealtime, a goat was bought and then tethered at the back of the hotel, and one of the busboys was appointed the official milker.

In another "special touch," in 1937 the CPR built a landing strip at the foot of Cascade Mountain to accommodate jazz musician Benny Goodman. Goodman had written to say he'd like to visit the hotel but would do so only if there was a place to land his plane. The CPR arranged to have a landing strip levelled and cleared at the base of Cascade Mountain. Goodman kept his end of the bargain, and most of the town turned out to watch one of the first airplanes land in the Bow Valley.

Goodman, of course, was only one of a great number of celebrities to visit the hotel during the golden years. Comedian Jack Benny tipped the staff with American silver dollars, which was about the best type of tip available in those days. Mickey Rooney, then involved in the Andy Hardy series, was turned down by an underinformed debutante when he asked her to dance. Cole Porter, Gracie Fields, and Henry Fonda—the list is long—were other well-known names who spent time at the hotel.

The 1930s were the heyday of press-agentry, when publicists sought to create photos so zany and offbeat that major publications would feel compelled to print them. Thus, newspapers and magazines were filled with starlets sitting on ice blocks during hot weather, or attempting to drive golf balls with an eight-metre-long club from the back of an elephant. In the case of the Banff Springs Hotel, the promotion of place and personality worked hand in glove, leading to photographs of well-known radio actor and dramatist Tommy Tweed playing the Banff Springs Golf Course in a suit of armour and Ginger Rogers perched outside on a small boulder sketching a Stoney chief.

This photo of actress Ginger Rogers sketching a Stoney Chief was typical of the eye-catching images used to promote the hotel in the 1930s.

The motion-picture industry also provided wonderful publicity for the hotel. In one notable example, the director of *49th Parallel*—an expensive British pro-Empire, anti-German war drama starring Leslie Howard and Laurence Olivier—

used the hotel's courtyard during Banff Indian Days as the setting for a dramatic confrontation between the Mounties and three Nazi U-boat crew members. The scene remains a favourite of Banff locals familiar with the Rockies' rich cinema history.

Yet another sort of publicity—this time literary—came after James Ramsey Ullman, the well-known writer of mountaineering tales, spent his first honeymoon at the hotel in 1927. During his stay he climbed in the Lake Louise area with Rudolph Aemmer, a renowned Swiss guide. Ullman's experiences with Aemmer were an inspiration, years later, for the *The White Tower*, which became the fourth-best-selling novel in the US in 1945.

The most entertaining moments at the hotel didn't always involve well-known celebrities. A particular maharaja, for example, arrived one summer during the mid-1930s with an entourage of about 30. He rented two or three of the larger suites and made it clear he wanted his stay to be memorably lavish. The staff didn't blink a collective eye when he ordered two double beds be pushed together, but a certain amount of amusement circulated when it was discovered the potentate was using the two beds solely for his own comfort and his wives were sleeping on the floor.

During the maharaja's visit, the lock on the royal jewel box was jammed shut. The hotel sent up an electrician to see if he could remedy the problem. The box was beautiful, inlaid with gems and jewels, but its lock was a cheap one—the sort that could be opened with a bobby pin. Realizing that if he opened the box at once it would probably be taken away before he got a chance to peek inside, the electrician-cum-locksmith pretended to struggle with the lock, hoping the assembled onlookers would eventually lose interest. The ploy worked, and as the audience drifted away, he lifted the lid and quickly peered

The Duke and Duchess of Windsor in the Banff Springs Hotel courtyard, 1941.

inside. The only jewel in the box, he later recalled, was a big surprise: a single rumpled copy of the Calcutta racing news.

Another distinguished hotel visitor in this era was the Prince of Wales. The prince was particularly fond of Alberta—so much so that on his first visit in 1919 he bought a ranch south of Calgary. Whenever he visited his ranch, he also spent time Banff, and it was rumoured that every local young woman knew in her heart of hearts that *she* was the proper mate for the royal bachelor. While some of the young swains countered that the requisite of royal courtship was royal blood, in 1936 the prince proved them wrong by abdicating the throne to marry American socialite Wallis Simpson. Four years later, as the Duke and Duchess of Windsor, they returned for the first of many visits to Alberta,

King George VI and Queen Elizabeth I stayed at the Banff Springs Hotel in 1939 (pictured above with William Lyon Mackenzie King). While in Banff, they gracefully consented to stop in for tea at the house of their Banff chauffeur, Jim Brewster (below). It is a matter of local historical humour that Jim, in his enthusiasm, failed to inform his wife of the plan, and arrived unannounced with the King and Queen of England.

his ranch, and the Banff Springs Hotel, as a couple.

In May 1939, King George VI and Queen Elizabeth stopped in Banff on their transcontinental tour. Canada's prime minister, William Lyon Mackenzie King, was with them, filling out the most important triumvirate ever to visit the hotel. The king and queen and their entourage had the entire hotel to themselves for two days, and management was able to concentrate its considerable resources on the couple. One of the special touches involved placing huge bouquets of wildflowers throughout the building, something the queen noted with appreciation.

There were other, earthier, guests. Most of the staff who worked at the hotel through the 1930s remembered Miss Steele, an elderly woman who arrived at the hotel every summer with rolls of two-inch medical tape, which she used to seal off all the windows and doors to her room. This was evidently to prevent any stray wisp of smoke from drifting into her room. Cigarette smokers, she was sure, were trying to poison her. In the dining room, she would take her meals as far away as possible from other diners and, much to the annoyance of her servers, would immediately move somewhere else if anyone she thought might be a smoker chose an adjoining table.

Although wealthy, Miss Steele was instantly recognizable around the hotel by the very old, very tattered brown coat she wore. She finally earned her spot in the Banff Springs Staff's Hall of Infamy one summer by leaving a small bag of candies as a tip for the housekeeper who had looked after her hermetically sealed

The Banff Springs Hotel from Surprise Corner in the early 1930s.

room all season. “But I wouldn’t eat them, dear,” she told the girl, presenting her with the rumpled brown paper bag. “I think they’ve got worms in them.”

Luckier than the young housekeeper was one of the drivers for the Brewster Company, the local transport outfit that enjoyed a long and profitable relationship with the hotel. As a Brewster driver, the young man was hired by a middle-aged guest to be her personal chauffeur for the summer. The woman became fond of the driver and at season’s end asked if he would drive her home to San Francisco. The fellow agreed, and the two left for California. When she finally and reluctantly said goodbye, she presented him with a cheque for $1,500, a sum that was to pay for his college education.

The staff itself was a strictly professional outfit in those days, and the same individuals who worked at the Banff Springs in the summer would spend the winter at the great resorts in California, Hawaii, Bermuda, and Florida. As the Great Depression settled in, they became increasingly dedicated to their work.

One of the best remembered of the golden years’ staff was a diminutive and charming maître d’ named Oscar Wulliman, who seemed predestined to serve in the great dining rooms of the continent. As a testament to Wulliman’s capabilities, the King of Siam insisted that he accompany him as his personal waiter from Banff to Victoria and, once there, tried to hire him on a permanent basis.

Wulliman, though, returned to the hotel, where his dedication to the cause of elegant dining was demonstrated as he was serving a private dinner party for the visiting Reynolds (of Reynolds Tobacco fame) family. Mr. Reynolds had caught a prize trout, which, per the hotel’s tradition, was exhibited in the lobby during the day. That night, the fish was stuffed, garnished, and baked to order, and Wulliman entered the dining room with the fish held high on a silver platter. Unfortunately, a pat of butter that had been dropped on the steps leading into the room took down Wulliman and the fish with a crash. Ever the professional, Oscar pieced the fish together and proceeded to the Reynoldses’ table, where he served the meal as best he could. It was only when he got back to the kitchen that he revealed his serving had been done with only one arm—the other had been broken in the fall.

Another well-remembered employee was a chef named Robert. Robert was as bad-tempered and spiteful as Wulliman was charming. He threw pots and pans around the kitchen, hurled carving knives at helpers, and, eventually, reaped at least some of what he had sown. One evening, walking past the still room (the area where specialty items such as fancy desserts were prepared), Robert made a passing comment to a young employee who was working on the far side of a long counter. The girl replied flippantly, and Robert exploded. Brandishing a large spoon, he leaped into the room, vaulted over the top of the counter, and landed ingloriously in 360 dessert dishes of Jell-O, each topped with whipped cream and one-quarter of a maraschino cherry.

Despite such “downstairs” occurrences, the hotel did a wonderful job of maintaining its “upstairs” atmosphere of cultured decorum. Full formal attire was de rigueur for the evening concerts and dances, and no gentleman would dare approach the dining room without a tie and jacket. No less a personage than Lady Diana Cooper, the wife of a prominent British politician, was refused entrance to the Alhambra Dining Room when she appeared at the door one day in her blue jeans, just back from a long trip on the trail.

The Cascade Ballroom was a social hub for guests in the 1930s.

There was one spot, though, where Lady Cooper would have been warmly welcomed in whatever she chose to wear. Sam's Place, a small Chinese restaurant that stood where the hotel's parkade is today, was officially a restaurant for Brewster packers and drivers. Unofficially, it was a meeting ground for Brewster cowboys, hotel staff, and guests alike. In time, it became as much a part of the hotel experience as the evening dance. Sam's was known as *the place* for anyone interested in having a good meal and a good time after the hotel's kitchens closed for the evening. By 11 p.m. on any given summer's evening, the small building would be packed with an interesting assortment of individuals. Cowboys could run through their routines with an eye on the brunette debutante in the corner, and the chambermaids could at last put their elbows on the counter and talk to the suave young men in tuxedos.

All golden moments, being but moments, have their end. By 1940, the impact of World War II was being felt across Canada, and Banff, a resort town, was particularly affected by what was happening to the rest of the nation. For the Banff Springs Hotel, war-related restraints on money and travel meant not only the loss of European patronage, but also a severe contraction of North American tourism. In 1942, management made the painful decision to close the hotel's doors for the duration of the war. In doing so, they had no idea they were also closing out the greatest era in the hotel's history. The doors would eventually reopen, but to a very different world.

Formerly the Presidential Suite, today's Royal Suite occupies parts of three floors and offers unparalleled views.

Tribulations and Triumph

"A GRAND OLD HOTEL WENDING ITS WAY THROUGH THE AGE OF AQUARIUS."

Just as the Great War transformed society, and thus the Banff Springs Hotel, World War II wrought dramatic change a quarter-century later. A shifting economy and an increasingly mobile and moneyed middle class challenged the viability of an institution designed and managed for society's elites.

The first stirrings of change were noticeable in the years just prior to the hotel's closing in 1942, when it began to cater to regularly scheduled train tours. Moderate in price, the popular trips commenced in the cities of Eastern Canada and operated on an itinerary that typically included a night or two at the Banff Springs Hotel.

That was just the beginning. The increased mobility and decreased costs of travel that came with the postwar economic boom revolutionized tourism. More North Americans owned cars than ever before, and the motoring public was infatuated with automobile travel and the industry that quickly emerged to service it. Every year saw more and better roads, and many of them, it seems, led to Banff. (Although, as one disgruntled but nostalgically hopeful guest from an earlier era observed, "just as many of them led away!") Commercial aviation, with its potential to transform tourism, was also beginning to have an impact.

In sum, the combination of mobility, accessibility, and the availability of more money changed the entire context of the hotel experience. The old clientele still visited, to be sure, spending their summers at the Banff Springs and the Château Lake

A 1940s CPR advertisement for the hotel.

Moxie Whitney and his big band were Banff Springs regulars in the 1950s.

Louise, and celebrities still flocked to the hotel. For years, Banffites told the story of bellboys flipping coins to see who would push Marilyn Monroe around in her wheelchair in 1953 after she twisted her ankle filming *River of No Return*. But year by year, season by season, a higher percentage of the hotel's total revenue came from short-stay, tour-scheduled guests.

It was only a matter of time until the middle class replaced the upper class as the hotel's "ruling class," and the hotel did its best to adjust to the new reality. For instance, the trend towards a less-starched propriety that had begun following the Great War gained momentum. Dress for concert and dance slipped from formal to semiformal, and the occasional gentleman was seen sans tie in the dining room.

Still, the hotel managed to hold on to, and even expand, many of its traditions. A radio broadcasting room was installed in the centre tower, and for many years Canadians across the country could tune in nightly to the big-band arrangements of Mart Kenney or Moxie Whitney. Old-timers still remember and recite the program introduction: "From the spacious ballroom of the Banff Springs Hotel, situated mile-high in the Canadian Rockies . . ."

The opening of the Trans-Canada Highway at Rogers Pass in July 1962 provided another big boost to "rubber tire tourism." By the mid-1960s, bus tours—a relaxed, reasonably priced alternative to automobile travel—were becoming a big part of the hotel's business. The trend to tours was further encouraged by the 1973 international oil crises, and by mid-decade the hotel was catering almost exclusively to bus tours, automobile-oriented families, and conventions. The days of the private coach on the mainline had become a distant memory.

One of the most significant consequences of better, faster, and more affordable transportation was the development of a ski season in Banff. As all-season travel became possible, the Banff ski hill owners were able to expand their markets from local to regional, and by the late 1960s Banff was on the threshold of becoming the winter resort it had dreamed about becoming for six decades. For the Banff Springs Hotel, the new development meant it was finally able to fulfill its own long-standing ambition. On December 5, 1969, it opened its doors to a winter clientele.

MEMORIES OF MARILYN

In the annals of Banff Springs' celebrity, only the visits of British royalty can rival the appearance of Marilyn Monroe. She arrived as a rising young star in August 1953 as part of the cast of *River of No Return*, a Western directed by Otto Preminger and costarring Robert Mitchum. The Canadian Rockies had been chosen as a location specifically to showcase the latest whizbang movie technology: wide-screen CinemaScope.

Monroe's visit was memorable on several counts. During the first part of the shoot, in Jasper, she was exiled from the Jasper Park Lodge for being "inappropriately" dressed in the dining room on several occasions. To add injury to insult, she sprained her ankle and had to resort to crutches to get around. And finally, to make matters even worse, she and Preminger did not get along—at all. Preminger opined that Monroe "had no talent as an actress," and Monroe dubbed Preminger's film, despite her starring role, as "a grade-Z cowboy movie." That left Mitchum to play peacemaker, but Mitchum was having issues of his own, worrying about a prolonged separation from his Hollywood peers, fans, and cronies. "Do they talk about us in Hollywood?" he said. "Do they know we're up here, or have they forgotten our existence?" He took to calling the movie *The Picture of No Return*.

Despite the difficulties on set, Monroe is remembered fondly by those who looked after her at the hotel. They referred to her as "friendly," "kind," and "a good sport." The latter description came into particular play after the cast had relocated to Banff and Monroe retwisted her ankle, landing her in the wheelchair over which the bellboys squabbled for pushing rights. Her mood was no doubt improved by a visit from Joe DiMaggio, her soon-to-be husband at the time.

As evidence of Monroe's enduring celebrity, guests still ask about her visit and, on occasion, try to book the room she stayed in. (The staff tradition is to keep the number of the room a secret.) However, a small plaque on the golf course commemorates her visit. It identifies the location as both that of Banff National Park's first campground and the site of Monroe's dressing trailer while she was in Banff.

The opening presented a few challenges. The hotel had none of the hallmark trappings of successful ski hotels; it was showing its age to the point of decrepitude; and the CPR management, which had flourished in its role as provider to the upper crust, seemed uncertain as to what to offer a middle class that was more interested in trendy new motor inns and intimate little ski chalets than grand old institutions. Innovation, inspiration, renovation, and even basic upkeep faltered in the postwar years.

To complicate the issue, the CPR had been growing and diversifying other pieces of its enterprise and by then had multiple subsidiaries running as company divisions. The hotels, comprising a small fraction of the overall operation, had little corporate presence or influence. Rumours spread that the hotels, and especially those at Banff and Lake Louise, were losing money. The board was looking for a buyer and, worse yet, was thinking about writing off the castle and tearing it down.

As a result, the first few years of the winter operation were not particularly happy ones. David Bayne, who worked for 42 years at the Banff Springs and the Château Lake Louise in capacities ranging from houseman to resident manager at the Springs and general manager at Lake Louise, remembers that often there were so few winter guests at the Banff Springs that he found himself being doorman, porter, front-desk clerk, bellman, and elevator operator for the same people. "There were almost no people at the hotel during the middle of the weeks," he said. "And half of the ones who were there were the entertainers." (One early bright spot, Bayne recalls, involved a couple of those entertainers, a duo of young females named Shirley and Judy, who played on a revolving stage in the Riverview Lounge. They packed the place, making the hotel a wildly popular weekend party spot.)

The overnight guests who did find their way to the hotel found themselves questioning their decision. During the first winter, one visitor compared his accommodation with his old college dorm room. Further, because the hotel was not fully winterized, parkas became an unofficial part of the dress code in the lounges and restaurants on cold, windy evenings.

Obviously, the Banff Springs, with few guests, faltering profits, failing infrastructure, peeling paint, and crumbling plaster, needed someone to take up its cause.

The castle found its white knight in the form of a Czech-born hotelier named Ivor Petrak. Hired in 1971 as general manager, Petrak brought to the hotel not only a strong background in international hotel management, but also an intimate working knowledge of the ski industry. In the seven years prior to coming to Banff, he had worked in four countries and managed five top-tier hotels, including the Trapp Family Lodge in Stowe, Vermont. Of equal importance was his finely tuned appreciation of both the Banff Springs' history and its founder. This appreciation dated back to 1951, when he worked for a short while at the Château Lake Louise. Petrak was determined to restore the Banff Springs to its former grandeur in a contemporary, year-round context. He was fond of saying "Van Horne had the vision and I have the mission."

Accordingly, he went to work, beginning with the CPR board of directors. He convinced them that a properly managed and maintained "grand hotel" could flourish in a middle-class economy. His own commitment to the project was total.

It wasn't until 1969 that the Banff Springs Hotel began opening for the winter season, allowing guests to enjoy a magical time of year in the Canadian Rockies.

A second early target was the Banff ski hill owners, to whom Petrak preached a sermon of competition: they would never run more than backyard ski hills for Calgarians, he told them, unless they learned to compete with the big resorts of North America and Europe. To get started, he said, Banff needed a "seamless ski experience," something that could be promoted as an inclusive ski package with accommodation, transportation to the ski lifts, lift tickets, and a rewarding après-ski experience. According to an associate, "Petrak saw a huge opportunity for Banff and the hotel, and he was determined to create an

A GHOSTLY HERITAGE

What's a castle without a ghost or two?

One of the more haunting aspects of the Petrak era concerns the ghosts who are rumoured to roam the castle's corridors. Some of the more ghost-appreciative staff of the 1970s and 1980s worried that the extensive, ongoing renovations of those decades would lead to a general dispersal of the hotel's spectral souls.

These stairs may be haunted by the ghost bride.

Such fears proved unfounded, however, as the favourite phantoms continued to appear, and a new one was even added to the roster.

By far the best known of the apparitions is the ghost bride, the spirit of a young, just-wed woman who died on the circular staircase that descends from the Cascade Ballroom. According to one version of the story, the bride was descending the stairs to join the wedding party when a candle from one of the candelabras that had been placed on the steps for romantic effect set the train of her wedding dress on fire. Trying to extinguish the flames, she toppled and fell, breaking her neck.

While no notice of such a death appears in the papers from the late 1920s or the 1930s—when the incident allegedly occurred—the lack of evidence has not stopped sundry staff and guests from reporting late-night sightings of an ethereal young female in a bridal veil either descending the stairs or dancing in the Cascade Ballroom. During the 1980s, there were even reports of numerous ghosts in elegant evening dress—evidently the wedding party—circulating about the old Rob Roy Room (an earlier iteration of today's Vermillion Room).

After years languishing in the obscurity of hotel staff folklore, the ghost bride achieved national recognition in 2014, when Canada Post and the Royal Canadian Mint selected her to be part of a Haunted Canada stamp and coin internationally successful winter resort even if it meant dragging both the hotel and town kicking and screaming to the finish line."

Petrak saw himself, at least in part, as a latter-day Van Horne. He certainly shared some of Van Horne's attributes. A bear-like man with a deep, rumbling voice and a strong Czech accent, he is remembered as a patriarch with a complex personality that was by turns autocratic, irascible, unpredictable, and, turning the coin, charismatically charming. As one employee said, "If Mr. P. likes you, he likes you. If he doesn't, he'll throw you out

GHOST BRIDE / MARIÉE FANTÔME BANFF SPRINGS, AB

collection. A commemorative plaque at the foot of the fatal staircase retells the story and provides information about both the stamp and the 25-cent coin. The bride's eyes open and the candles along the staircase light up when the coin is tilted. According to the Mint, the collection "helped bring the ghost bride's story out of the shadows and allowed her spirit to live on beyond the walls of this hotel as part of our shared Canadian heritage."

The latest addition to the hotel's resident ghost population dates to the late 1970s. As the story goes, after dinner one night, the wife of a convention delegate returned to the couple's room on the ninth floor to discover she had left the key with her husband many floors below. Using the guest phone near the elevators, she called the bell desk for help. The bellman hurried to help, but to his surprise, he arrived to find the woman not out in the hall but already settled comfortably in her room. She thanked him for his offer of assistance but said she had been already helped by an elderly man with a Scots accent in an older-style uniform. The description was of Sam McAuley, a deceased bell captain who had often remarked that, given the chance, he would come back to the hotel as a ghost after he died.

Aside from assisting guests with their locks, Sam's ghost—with a sly sense of humour—is known for hijacking the elevator and taking it to floors other than those desired. He also assists with luggage and, on occasion, appears at the bedside of guests on the ninth floor in the wee hours of the morning. According to long-term staff, Sam's spirit, in whatever form it takes, is very much an active, helpful presence in the hotel.

Sam and the ghost bride—and particularly the Royal Mint's recognition of the latter—have generated a whole new audience for the hotel. Responding to public demand following the stamp and coin's release, the hotel began running ghost tours several times a year. On a good night, such as Halloween, the tours can draw dozens of guests. To further celebrate the bride's new fame, the Vermillion Room sells a special Ghost Bride beer.

Ivor Petrak shows Canadian Prime Minister Pierre Trudeau through the hotel during a 1970s visit.

of his park." Even those he liked were never sure what he might do in next. A former bell captain remembers Petrak blowing up at him one day, absolutely furious that there weren't any ping-pong balls on the ping-pong table at the pools.

Whether they were in Mr. P.'s park or not, very few who knew him would deny he was the right person for the task at hand. He was entrepreneurial, resourceful, and ferociously determined—all traits that over the years helped him not only renew the hotel but also dramatically expand and develop the property and open new and much-needed markets. Aside from being the Banff Springs Hotel's general manager, Petrak was also regional vice president for CP Hotels' mountain region, in which role he helped build a portfolio of Canadian Rockies properties that eventually included the Banff Springs Hotel, the Château Lake Louise, Jasper Park Lodge, and the Lodge at Kananaskis.

Marilyn Bell, who worked for the hotel for 34 years in both operations and sales and served as Petrak's executive assistant for many years, recalls that while Petrak was initially hired to oversee the winter operation, it didn't take long for him to develop a comprehensive master plan for the hotel that was thereafter constantly evolving. "Once he had an idea, he never let anything stand in his way of making it happen. He would beg, borrow, steal and make deals with the devil to get the work done."

To win support for his grand scheme, Petrak worked with everyone—CP executives, Parks Canada, Travel Alberta and all the other marketing groups, the Town of Banff, outside organizations, and others. According to Bell, this "allowed him to work miracles inside the organization." (Bell herself was no slouch when it came to networking and working miracles. One colleague remembers her as a nurturing "queen of the castle" who knew all the players, kept track of all the pieces, and kept the big projects moving ahead.)

Having talked the board into making a preliminary investment in the hotel's revival, Petrak began reworking the property in a process that would continue under two general managers for nearly 30 years.

He began with the task he was hired to do. He winterized the hotel and its infrastructure, ignoring the naysayers who said it couldn't be done. He created new, intimate spaces and bars that fit the winter market. He converted the old Garden Lounge into a cozy dining club and lounge called the Rob Roy Room (which later became the Bow Valley Grill and later yet the Vermillion Room—both very different iterations of the Rob Roy Room), and built a cabaret in the downstairs arcade (now the lobby level).

It was at some point in the early 1970s that the hotel, complete with après-ski lounges, rock bands, and a decidedly younger crowd, acquired a new status and a new direction—a grand old dame wending her way through the Age of Aquarius.

Petrak wasn't just thinking of the winter, though. As part of his efforts to create a more welcoming facility for all seasons, he immediately began to upgrade the guest rooms. In his first year, he repainted and refurnished 75 rooms on the ninth floor. Thereafter, he redid 150 rooms a year—carpentry, painting, bedspreads, and upholstery—drawing heavily on the sensibilities and inspiration of Lazlo Funtek, a respected theatre-set designer from the Banff Centre. In 1975, Petrak had the hotel and elevators rewired for $20 million and three years later updated the plumbing for another $15 million. He also reworked the arcade level a second time, creating space for a number of boutiques and restaurants.

While the board was generous in providing funding for infrastructure upgrades and, later, major redevelopment projects, it was tightfisted when it came to furnishings and décor. Given the scope of Petrak's ambitions, there was never enough money, so his resourcefulness came into play. For example, by bestowing favours on CP executives and other hotel managers, he was able to wrangle used furniture and fixtures from their properties—to the degree that housekeeping employees informally named some of the room designs after the hotels their furniture had come from. Thus they would speak of the hotel's "early Royal York," "Empress," and "Château Frontenac" décors.

Beyond the furniture and fixtures, though, Petrak made some acquisitions that, in less genteel circles, would give him bragging rights as a world-class scrounger. One was an entire English-pub-style bar—right down to the stools, booths, and shelf knickknacks—that he picked up from the Calgary Tower when it was renovating the tower's bar. Moved to Banff, the bar became the Waldhaus Restaurant and Pub, located in what was formerly the golf course clubhouse.

Another famous procurement was the massive crystal chandelier that today illuminates the Oval Room (just outside the Cascade Ballroom). When Petrak learned the fixture was being removed from the ballroom of Edmonton's Château Lacombe as part

The Admiral's Suite [left] was one of many guest rooms Petrak had built in imaginative locations. It has since been removed, but the distinctive circular window [right] remains in the wall of an alcove off the Rundle Lounge.

of a renovation, he worked his contacts to convince the château to sell him the chandelier, which had an estimated market price of $20,000, for $100 plus the cost of shipping it to Banff. Comprising 3,000 pieces of fine Bavarian crystal, the fixture takes two staff members eight hours to clean.

Petrak was also skilled at ("obsessed with" might be more appropriate) converting empty hotel nooks and crannies into profitable guest rooms, suites, and public chambers. When, for instance, he discovered two bellboys taking a nap in an out-of-the-way cubbyhole (that the bellboys had used as a secluded retreat for years), Petrak roused them, declared the cubby wasted space, and turned it into a public washroom.

The bellboys, of course, disagreed with Petrak's judgment, as did the housekeepers who discovered their linen closets converted into a surround for a new whirlpool, and the housemen who found their banquet-chair-storage room turned into a part of the banquet room itself.

Another well-remembered conversion was one regarding an abandoned housekeeper's office. The office had been little more than idle air surrounding one of the hotel's old, unused staircases, but its awkward configuration didn't deter Petrak from turning it into one of the hotel's more interesting guest rooms. The new room featured a bedroom and sitting area separated by a wide set of stairs that swept majestically up to the bathroom—which featured a large jetted tub and one of the first bidets installed in the hotel.

Similarly, he converted a north wing attic (used for storage and overflow staff accommodation for as long as anyone could remember) into a string of eighth-floor guest rooms that today provide some of best views in the entire hotel. He also enclosed a balcony above the hotel entrance to create the Van Horne Room, which is known today, appropriately, as the Ivor Petrak Room.

Petrak's passion for efficiency extended to the hotel's operations as well. Shortly after arriving in Banff, he asked one of the seasoned porters to give him a tour of the property. When the porter revealed a special porter's elevator, Petrak saw an efficiency opportunity and quickly had it converted to an eight-storey laundry chute.

Those renovations, however, were only Petrak's opening salvo. In the fall of 1980, having been through the hotel once, he launched a new campaign to further upgrade all the rooms and public spaces. With the new winter season in mind, he also rebuilt the outside swimming pool, turning it into a welcoming hot pool for muscle-weary skiers.

By 1982, more than $60 million had gone into modernizing the hotel's infrastructure and refurbishing its rooms, and still Petrak showed no sign of slowing down. In 1985, with the backing of fellow visionary William Stinson (who was appointed CPR president in 1981 and CEO in 1985), Petrak initiated an elaborate two-phase expansion that

A 1985 aerial view of the hotel, before the addition of the conference centre and dedicated staff accommodation. The town of Banff can be seen across the river, top right.

The Manor Highland Wing (top), now part of what is called the Gatehouse, was designed to blend seamlessly with the main hotel building, and was connected by a raised walkway (above).

Parks Canada had approved nearly a decade earlier. One convincing argument for the expansion was that it would position the Banff Springs to profit handsomely from the fast-approaching Calgary-hosted XV Winter Olympic Games.

With a budget of $37.5 million, the first phase entailed yet more additions and conversions. For starters, the Lower Annex, the Upper Annex, and the Château Ramsay—all constructed following the 1926 fire and used primarily as staff accommodation during the intervening decades—were linked together and converted into a 246-room guest wing that included its own lobby and lounge. While the Lower Annex kept its old Tudor exterior, the rest of the complex was faced with Rundlestone to align it visually with the rest of the property. As well, a Plus-15 walkway gave it a direct, elevated connection to the main hotel. Collectively, the new configuration was named the Manor Highland Wing (now known as the Gatehouse).

The staff, in turn, were moved into 336 new apartments built to the west of the hotel, across Spray Avenue. Constructed of stacked mobile units, the innovative arrangement, said Petrak, constituted "the best staff accommodation in the world." Managers did even better with their 35 new townhouses. To help finance the new housing, part of the original CPR lease lands were subdivided and sold as 22 Banff townsite lots.

In the hotel proper, cozy little two-floor honeymoon suites, complete with spiral staircases, heart-shaped headboards, and Jacuzzis, were tucked into the uppermost tower turrets, and the hotel's largest and most luxurious suite, which Petrak named the Presidential, was fashioned from staff quarters and the hotel's old water tank on the tenth, eleventh, and twelfth floors. Opened in December 1986, the suite featured marble, brass, and plush fabrics throughout, a glass elevator to carry guests from floor to floor, eight bedrooms with canopied beds and ornate original wall tapestries, a reception foyer with a fireplace, private concierge service, a sauna, a lap pool (supported by the structural underpinnings that once braced the water tank), and a multilevel living room with a baby grand piano, loft library, stereo system, and large-screen television.

Today, known as the Royal Suite, the rooms of the former Presidential Suite still command the best views in the house. And of all the views, perhaps the very best is afforded by a toilet wedged into a little corner of one of the bathrooms, which offers a glorious, unimpeded overlook of the confluence of the Bow and Spray Rivers—the old "million dollar view." Because of the awkward configuration of the turret corner in which it sits, the toilet took carpenters and plumbers nearly three days to install, but the view from its seat alone nearly justifies the price: up to $5,000 a night.

With the Olympics approaching, it was no coincidence that the suite's first occupant was Donald Barr, then publisher of *Sports Illustrated* magazine. In a marketing coup, Petrak and his team sold the magazine on using the hotel as an incentive destination for its advertisers. The result was 250 rooms booked nightly for the week before the Olympics, for the 16 days of the Olympics, and for the week following the Olympics. The hotel was also used as the venue for all of the publication's executive management and board meetings for the two years prior to the Olympics.

Incidentally, *Sports Illustrated* would return to the hotel in July 2010 with a crew of 20 for a closely guarded photo shoot. The results of the shoot appeared in the magazine's

The Banff Springs Golf Course Clubhouse has a unique hexagonal design.

2011 swimsuit issue. Kim Glass, one of the three model-athletes who braved maximum exposure to the mountain winds and glacier-fed waters, fell in love with Banff National Park, calling it "God's own work of art" in her social media account of the experience.

Golf course renovation was another part of the redevelopment. By the 1980s, the course was being played by record numbers of golfers, and was showing signs of wear and tear. The clubhouse needed expanding, the driving range needed lengthening, and parking—a headache for all concerned—needed rethinking. Never one for half measures, Petrak responded by building a $3 million, 30,000-square-foot clubhouse and adding an additional nine holes, the Tunnel Mountain 9, in the centre of the course. The new clubhouse, employing a radical hexagonal design inspired by a tepee, featured large windows and a wraparound deck that made the most of the surrounding scenery. The old stone clubhouse, located immediately below the hotel to the east, was converted to the Waldhaus Restaurant and Pub.

To be successful, Petrak's long campaign to bring the hotel back from the brink demanded more than new rooms, new paint, and a new clubhouse. It needed to be promoted and marketed to new audiences in new ways. "Marketing was a major part of Petrak's plan," said Marilyn Bell. "And he had a gift for it." He pushed hard to increase the number of bus tours that stopped at the hotel as well the number of groups that used the hotel as a destination for incentive trips for high-performing employees. He promoted the hotel as a prime convention site to increase its meeting business. He wooed the new winter ski trade with special package deals, including rooms for as low as $14 a night, and by hiring an internationally recognized French-ski-team star, Audrey de Baghy, to promote them. He also looked to Canadian Pacific Air Lines and its international routes for new markets, which brought Mexico and an entirely new audience into the hotel's orbit.

And then, during a visit to Frankfurt in 1972, Petrak noticed the number of Japanese tourists flocking to Germany and thought, "Why not Banff?" Returning to Canada, he recruited a marketing prodigy named Jean Cimon to create a Japan campaign. Cimon—who was fully up for the assignment and who, most helpfully, had a Japanese wife—finagled an appearance on Japan's most popular TV talk show. Hosted by Kai Ohashi and billed as Japan's Johnny Carson show, it had a huge following, and it soon became evident that Cimon's appearance had been a spectacular success. With strategic transportation support from Canadian Pacific Air Lines and a number of enterprising tour companies, Japanese tourism to Western Canada, and to Banff in particular, rose from a trickle in the 1960s to what older Banffites today recall as the "Japanese invasion" of the 1970s. So popular was Banff with its new audience that the hotel became the location for a Japanese prime-time television soap opera named *Rice Curry*.

Petrak's marketing efforts received another boost in 1984, when the UNESCO World Heritage Centre created a Canadian Rocky

WORLD-CLASS ROCKIES RECOGNITION

As part of its efforts to promote peace and security through international collaboration, the United Nations Educational, Scientific and Cultural Organization (UNESCO) identifies, recognizes, and secures the world's great cultural and natural heritage sites.

In 1984, the UNESCO World Heritage Committee accepted Canada's proposal that the four mountain national parks of Banff, Jasper, Yoho, and Kootenay be added to the list of World Heritage Sites as the Canadian Rocky Mountain Parks World Heritage Site. In 1990, three adjoining BC provincial parks—Mount Robson, Mount Assiniboine, and Hamber—joined the national parks as part of the site.

UNESCO's Statement of Significance for the site reads as follows:

Renowned for their scenic splendor, the Canadian Rocky Mountain Parks . . . exemplify the outstanding physical features of the Rocky Mountain Biogeographical Province. Classic illustrations of glacial geological processes—including icefields, remnant valley glaciers, canyons and exceptional examples of erosion and deposition—are found throughout the area. The Burgess Shale Cambrian and nearby Precambrian sites contain important information about the earth's evolution.

Peyto Lake, one of the best known natural features of the Canadian Rocky Mountain Parks World Heritage Site.

Indira Gandhi is welcomed to the hotel by Ivor Petrak.

Mountain Parks World Heritage Site comprising Banff, Jasper, Kootenay, and Yoho National Parks. The designation allowed the hotel to begin to think of itself not only as a gateway to Canada's first national park, but also to a site of international significance.

As Petrak had promised, his renovations and determined marketing reinvigorated the hotel. By 1990, business was booming in summer and winter, and the list of royals, politicians, and celebrities who had visited through the 1970s and 1980s would have made Van Horne proud. Among them were prime ministers Pierre Trudeau, Joe Clark, and Brian Mulroney, as well as Lord Mountbatten, Prince Philip, Princess Alexandria, the Duke and Duchess of Kent, Margaret Thatcher, Mikhail Gorbachev, Indira Gandhi, Prince Norihito and Princess Takamatsu, Prince Rainier, Arnold Schwarzenegger, and Maria Shriver.

As in the past, the presence of celebrities added to the store of cherished hotel anecdotes. David "Mo" Moberg, who worked at the hotel for 51 years, starting as a printer in 1962 and moving on to become head porter, bell captain, and eventually manager of guest relations, recalls Prince Philip and part of his entourage stepping into an elevator one day to encounter a chipper, chatty, and obviously unwitting elevator attendant. After greetings and pleasantries about the weather had been exchanged, the young woman smiled at the prince and asked, "And what do you do when you're not staying with us?"

"Actually," replied a bemused Prince Philip, "I'm a prince."

"All right!" said the young lady, extending her hand. "And I'm the Queen of Sheba. Pleased to meet you."

Moberg was also treated to an impromptu golf lesson in the lobby of the hotel by Bob Hope, spent an afternoon fishing with Jack Lemmon, and smuggled Meg Ryan (among others) out through the porter's entrance so she could avoid the lobby. And he remembers greeting Lee Marvin at the doors of the hotel when Marvin was in town to shoot an eminently forgettable film named *Death Hunt*. Marvin was involved in a nasty palimony case at the time, and when Moberg asked politely if he could show Marvin to his room, the beleaguered actor replied, "No, you *cannot* show me to my room. You can show me to the bar."

Several repeat guests quickly became staff favourites. For example, Mrs. Tomiko Bjork, from Japan, was visiting Banff with her husband in 1969 when she looked down on the hotel from the Sulphur Mountain gondola. Enthralled, she visited the hotel, and returned as a guest in 1972—and thereafter each spring for the following 36 years. Delighting in high etiquette, she went out for dinner every year with a number of the hotel's department managers and always made a point of wearing a tiara, a long gown, and evening gloves. On her 88th birthday, her hotel friends hosted a special luncheon for her in the Rundle Lounge and presented her with a Fairmont Colleague name tag, making her an honorary Banff Springs Hotel staff member.

Regardless of his or her status, however—celebrity or non-celebrity, repeat visitor or one-night tourist—every guest shared a common thread that spooled back a hundred years. In 1988, as in 1888, the only tasks at hand were to recreate in the wild Canadian Rockies, luxuriate in a castle of dreams, and gather up a collection of cherished mountain memories.

Mrs. Tomiko Bjork with hotel managers on her 88th birthday.

The Banff Springs Hotel from the Spray Valley.

A Second Century

"WE DON'T SELL ROOMS. WE SELL DREAMS!"

In 1988, 100 years after welcoming its first guests, the Banff Springs Hotel was not only back on its feet, but was also one of the busiest hotels in Canada. There was no more corporate talk of a sale or teardown. Indeed, the CP hotels were being managed as a new standalone division that was acquiring new properties and establishing an international reputation. The hotel's 841 bedrooms, including 66 suites and 13 meeting rooms that could be converted to guest rooms as needed, could accommodate 1,750 guests on any given night. More to the point, the hotel was again delivering on the promises envisioned by Van Horne and Price: superlative service in luxurious accommodation, an expansive array of amenities, and a destination of unsurpassed physical beauty. That it was all packaged in a building designed to evoke an elegant, timeless, and romantic past gave Petrak one of his favourite lines: "Our guests are dreamers who want to live in castles. We don't sell rooms. We sell dreams!"

To acknowledge its centenary, the hotel hosted a series of events over the course of the year. Among other honours, the Banff Springs Hotel was recognized as a National Historic Site by the Historic Sites and Monuments Board of Canada. Dated March 22, 1988, the citation names the Banff Springs as an outstanding example of a large-scale resort hotel in a natural setting that became "a symbol of tourism in the Canadian Rockies." The hotel is noted for its "restrained Chateau-style design and Arts-and-Crafts finishes and forms," "the distinctive décor of its interior spaces," and the views of the surrounding mountain landscape and of the hotel itself within that landscape.

On May 31, an official recognition of the anniversary was held in Mount Stephen Hall. All of the hotel's living resident and general managers, of whom there were seven, were brought to Banff by train from Calgary and then transported to the hotel by horse and buggy. Other dignitaries included David Day, the superintendent of Banff National Park, acting as master of ceremonies; Robert DeMone, the president, chairman, and chief executive officer of the Canadian Pacific Hotels Corporation; and Thomas McMillan, the federal environment minister. Jon Whyte, a curator for the Whyte Museum of the Canadian Rockies, spoke on "the Banff Springs Legend," after which DeMone and McMillan unveiled a commemorative plaque and signed a declaration of heritage preservation.

One of the other popular centenary events was a staff reunion, attended by over 250 former employees. The participants enjoyed reacquainting themselves with the hotel and former colleagues in a series of receptions, dinners, afternoon teas, tours, and bridge games. There was a memorabilia book and, according to Marilyn Bell, "We [the hotel] declared an amnesty for the return of artifacts that had been smuggled out of the hotel years or even decades ago as souvenirs of a summer in Banff. It was surprising to learn just how many of those souvenirs there actually were, and how many were returned." Cutlery, glasses, and small signs were common items.

THE BEST VIEWS IN THE VALLEY

According to its 1988 National Historic Site citation, the Banff Springs Hotel is distinguished not only by the views it offers of the surrounding mountainscape, but also by the way it aesthetically complements the mountainscape itself. While generations of photographers have laboured to find the best spot in the valley to capture the image of the castle against its mountain backdrop, five well-known locations never disappoint.

The view from the 14th hole of the golf course is a memorable one for golfers.

The Banff Springs Golf Course: The approach to the 14th green of the Banff Springs Golf Course offers one of the most famous views of the hotel. It is enjoyed and praised by generations of golfers from around the world.

The view from Surprise Corner.

Surprise Corner: The aptly named switchback where Buffalo Street meets Tunnel Mountain Drive is located on a high bluff directly above Bow Falls and just across the Bow River from the Banff Springs Hotel. Opposite the small Surprise Corner parking area, a flight of stairs leads to a log-sided interpretive viewpoint. The corner has been a favoured site for photographers since the earliest days of the hotel.

Sulphur Mountain: The Banff Gondola transports visitors from the end of Mountain Avenue to a 2,281-metre (7,484-foot) elevation near the summit of Sulphur Mountain. From the gondola's upper terminal, the Banff Springs, looking very much "the castle in the wilderness," rises prominently above the surrounding development.

Tunnel Mountain: There's no gondola to the summit of the "Sleeping Buffalo" (as the mountain is known traditionally to the Stoney Nakoda), but it's easily reached on foot in 45 minutes from St. Julien Road in the Banff townsite. The hotel comes into full view just below the summit. King George VI and Queen Elizabeth enjoyed the vista after hiking up the mountain in 1939 as part of the royal tour.

Mount Norquay: A small turnout at the last switchback on the Mount Norquay Road offers a fine cross-valley view of the Banff Springs rising majestically between Mount Rundle and Sulphur Mountain.

Looking down to the hotel from the top of Tunnel Mountain.

A reunion of Banff Springs' managers took place at the hotel's centenary celebration in 1988. The top row pictured from left to right is Don Williams, Cliff Watson, Ivor Petrak, Patrick Fitt, and Michael Broadhurst. Seated is Ron Deyell and Colin McCartney.

One might suppose a century of success would earn a hotel the right to rest on its laurels for a year or two, but this was not the case for the Banff Springs. Van Horne's old dictum about building railways—that is, if you're not moving full steam ahead, you're moving backwards—was equally applicable to the hotel's management of the day. Having spent millions in the 1970s and 1980s to recapture its former status, the hotel now sought millions more to maintain that status and remain relevant to a constantly evolving market. Accordingly, as the Banff Springs edged into its second 100 years, close to $100 million was budgeted to further modernize the facility and adapt its offerings to the changing needs of the vacation and convention market.

Of all the alterations, the biggest was the addition of the $25 million Banff Springs Conference Centre, which opened in November 1990. While the hotel had always hosted large functions, the new facility, with a footprint just shy of 3,200 square metres (34,000 square feet), unlocked a new world of opportunities. Indeed, combining the meeting and public function rooms in the main hotel with that of the new centre, the Banff Springs became the largest conference resort under one roof in Canada.

Backing onto the lower slopes of Sulphur Mountain, the centre looks northeast to the hotel. The architects—Carruthers, Marshall and Associates of Calgary—designed the curved two-storey structure to match the rest of the property with a Rundlestone façade (requiring almost one million kilograms of rock), a gabled roofline, and replica period furnishings. It includes four spacious function rooms, including the spacious Van Horne Ballroom (which can seat 1,600 delegates), 10 smaller meeting rooms, and a 252-seat theatre. There is also a conservatory, an area for outdoor gatherings, and a number of guest rooms and suites reserved for event organizers. High ceilings, removable chandeliers, and outsized rear access allow vehicles to drive into the main floor, and a cavernous finishing kitchen helps get meals that have been partially prepped in the hotel's main kitchen out to delegates in a timely fashion. Additional amenities include a well-equipped and fully wired business centre, a car-rental agency, a grocery store, a liquor store, and a sports clothing and bike rental outlet.

The Conference Centre, which opened in 1990, is anchored by the Van Horne Ballroom.

Of special note, there is also a bowling alley. In a throwback to the era when the hotel was willing to build a landing strip for Benny Goodman and buy a goat to provide Dr. Fowler with his mealtime milk, Petrak decided to build a bowling alley after he learned that the non-skiing wife of a skier had written to see if there was a bowling alley nearby. If there was, she wrote, she would pack her bowling ball for the trip and bowl while her husband skied. The request struck Petrak's fancy, and a bowling alley was added to the plans.

Justin Trudeau, future Canadian prime minister, with hotel manager David Roberts at the Fairmont Banff Springs Celebrity Sports Invitational.

To help celebrate the opening of the conference centre, the hotel teamed up with the Alberta government, Parks Canada, several local businesses, and a former child evangelist preacher turned actor turned charity promoter named Marjoe Gortner to host what was billed as the Banff Norquay Celebrity Ski Invitational. Produced by Gortner, the invitational brought celebrities together for a weekend of winter games to raise funds for African wildlife conservation. Held in January 1990, the event featured such stars of the day as Kris Kristofferson, Ali MacGraw, William Shatner, Angie Dickenson, Bruce Jenner, Roger Moore, Henry Mancini, and Jean-Claude Van Damme.

The master of ceremonies for the weekend gala dinner was Robin Leach, then host of the TV series *Lifestyles of the Rich and Famous*. Leach's appearance immediately led reporters to dub the Banff Springs the "Hotel of the Rich and Famous." And, in fact, it was just that for the next 22 Januarys. The event, with an evolving list of sponsors, became the Fairmont Banff Springs Celebrity Sports Invitational. In its later years, it became a focused five-day fundraiser for Robert F. Kennedy's Waterkeeper Alliance, a coalition of environmental groups dedicated to protecting North America's waterways, including the Bow River. Each year, the celebrities—all A-list stars—would head to the slopes of Sunshine Village to play in the snow, participate in various team competitions involving skis, snowboards, snowshoes, and toboggans, and mug for the press. Whether Justin Trudeau was arguing that his grand slalom race with Jason Priestley was really a photo finish, not a loss, or Robin Williams was improvising at the Rude Boys ski shop in Banff, the invitational garnered a lot of publicity—and a ton of money. In 2011, with individual tickets costing $500 and a "gold table" of $10,000, the black-tie gala raised $1 million for the alliance.

The conference centre was the last piece of Petrak's ambitious redevelopment program. In 1990, he resigned as general manager to assume duties with a newly created (1988) CPR division devoted solely to its hotels. Canadian Pacific Hotels and Resorts (aka CP Hotels) was mandated to expand the business, starting with the acquisition of hotels owned by the rival Canadian National Railway. Petrak, who had championed the creation of the division, was delighted that the hotels had finally found a home of their own and agreed to become vice president of resort development.

As it turned out, no one will ever know what the latter-day Van Horne might have done in his new role. Suddenly and unexpectedly, Petrak passed away a scant three weeks after his farewell party at the hotel. His legacy at the Banff Springs, however, was secure: during his 19-year tenure, he had fulfilled his dream of returning the Banff Springs Hotel to its former stature and, in so doing, welcomed a whole new generation of visitors.

While one might think there would be little left to work on following Petrak's extended frenzy of additions, conversions, renovations, and refurbishings, there was, in fact, much to do. Most of Petrak's energy, and the resources he'd scrambled to find, had been devoted to assembling the large structural pieces of his master plan, which included the Manor Highland Wing, the conference centre, the new staff accommodation, and the expanded golf course and new clubhouse. As Marilyn Bell says, "Petrak was focused on the big picture; he didn't have a lot of time to worry about the sockets in the guest rooms."

The detail work fell to Ted Kissane, Petrak's successor as the Banff Springs' general manager and CP regional vice president. Kissane was a very different person and a very different manager than Petrak, but, just as Petrak had been the right person for the hotel in the 1970s, Kissane was the right fit for the 1990s. At one time recognized as a bit of a hotelier boy wonder, he had been hired in his mid-20s to senior positions and gone on to be a successful long-term hospitality professional with deep ties to Sheraton Hotels and Resorts.

One of a new breed of "modern" managers, Kissane had a style based more on the contemporary themes of cooperation, teamwork, and individual empowerment than on old-school notions of command and control. He thoughtfully developed clear objectives and pursued them methodically with detailed plans. One associate remembers him as a "diplomatic, respectful and very capable" manager; another recalls "a visionary, a motivator, and a leader with a great sense of humour;" yet another praises him for his "wonderful ability to set employees up for success and then get out of the way."

No doubt it was with the idea of a successful beginning that—after a prehiring tour of the hotel—Kissane said he would become general manager only with a guarantee that he would have enough funding to finish, in fine detail, the pieces Petrak had assembled. CP Hotels chairman William Stinson, always a champion of the hotel, promised the money and further gave Kissane an ambitious mandate: to fully re-create the splendour and glory of the old turn-of-the-century Banff Springs Hotel.

Looking to top European resort hotels as his standard, and with an eye to attracting top European clientele, Kissane went to work. Among his priorities: rework the guest rooms from top to bottom; build the hotel's first modern spa; reconfigure the Manor Highland Wing; rebuild the main kitchen; restore the golf course to its old Stanley Thompson grandeur; and construct an entirely new entry hall and lobby. And, as part of the process, find new markets and modernize the hotel's culture with an emphasis on heritage and staff training.

Job one was to do something about the rooms. While Petrak had renewed and redecorated the guest rooms twice, he had done so with a limited budget and a lot of used furniture. The result was a mix-and-match décor that needed rethinking in light of a new generation of guests who were more discerning and expected more for their dollars. Kissane's first step was to do a rapid blanket renovation of all the rooms in the

An artist's rendering of the new spa facility, 1994.

hotel to bring them up to what he considered a minimally acceptable standard. ("They were all beautiful, and they were all blue," said a former manager.) Several years later, he went over them again, using, as one staff member put it, "a finer grade of sandpaper." It was expensive sandpaper, too—$33,000 was allocated for each room. Included in the cost were, at long last, new custom furniture, fine bed linens, artwork and wall coverings, decorative lighting, and granite and marble vanities and fixtures in the bathrooms.

Another of Kissane's early projects was to overhaul the hotel's pool operation. Decades earlier, the Sulphur Mountain hot springs had been Banff's springboard to fortune and fame, and as early as 1912 the Banff Springs Hotel was reported to have "the finest bathing establishment on the continent." Seeking to reclaim that reputation, Kissane turned to Europe for inspiration, envisioning an upscale oasis of pampered indulgence that could compete with a classic European spa yet be fully integrated with the rest of the hotel. At the time, Kissane's idea was a bold one: modern spas were still new in North America, and there was some question as to whether the board would back the venture. Much to Kissane's delight, the board voted for the grandest and most expensive of the three proposals he presented.

The result was the Solace Spa (now the Willow Stream Spa), which opened in 1995 as a 3,530-square-metre (38,000-square-foot) facility anchored by a large Romanesque mineral pool with room for 21 bathers.

The centrepiece of the Willow Stream Spa is this magnificent mineral pool.

Featuring a mosaic of green and blue tiles, salts and minerals imported from South Africa, an underwater sound system, and mood lighting, the pool is the spa's most popular attraction. "A soak in that pool," according to one obviously impressed guest, "is a blissful journey into serenity."

To one side of the mineral pool, a series of three waterfalls, each a different temperature, fill three private pools. Large windows provide a view to the outdoor whirlpool, which is especially popular on snowy winter days. Even the changerooms, complete with his and her lounging areas, fresh fruit, hot drinks, and daily newspapers, are memorably luxurious. The facilities also include a hair salon, a fitness centre, private inhalation rooms, saunas, and eucalyptus-infused steam rooms. With a constantly evolving program, the spa offers a full suite of massage therapies, aromatherapy, wraps, scrubs, manicures, pedicures, facials, and a "virtual fitness" service that is accessible 24 hours per day. Hearkening back to the 1912 reviews, the spa is consistently ranked among the best in Canada.

Another Kissane project, under the direction of Calgary architect Robert LeBlond and Calgary interior designer Kerry Busby, was to renovate and upgrade the Manor Highland Wing—the southern arm of the hotel that had been converted from staff housing to guest accommodation prior to the Olympics. According to David Bayne, former resident manager of the Banff Springs, the manor was originally meant to provide a midlevel hotel offering that would compete with the downtown Banff hotels. In fact, he says, "We quickly learned that a less expensive room option wasn't needed, or even wanted." The demand for the "full hotel experience" was such that many guests assigned to the manor rooms complained about them, mainly commenting they were too small.

Kissane's response was another bold proposal. He claimed that by using two of the old, smaller rooms to make one new, large room, he could end the complaints, build new customer loyalty, and, by charging higher rates, increase revenue. "Some of us were worried," says Marilyn Bell, "that the board would think Ted had been breathing too much mountain air."

Again, though, the board agreed to the investment. In 1997, the newly renovated Manor Highland Wing was unveiled, featuring larger guest rooms, new suites, and a new Scots baronial décor throughout. Kissane's big bet about complaints and loyalty paid off: the complaints were replaced by compliments from guests wanting to return, and the hotel—despite losing 76 rooms to the manor reconfiguration—turned a profit on its investment. (The Manor Highland Wing was later renamed the Stanley Thompson Wing and, more recently, the Gatehouse.)

Golf remained an unwaveringly popular activity at the hotel, and the course's reputation as one of the continent's great "fair challenges" continued to grow. Over the years, however, Stanley Thompson's original design had been subjected to multiple changes, and the turf had suffered from long snow-covered winters and summer traffic that included not only multitudes of humans but also herds of elk. Beginning in 1994 and then in 1998 and 1999, golf course architects from the US and Canada used photographs and other historic reference materials to resurrect the entire Stanley Thompson course. Fairways and greens were planted with vintage grasses, and new tee boxes were constructed to keep Thompson's "shot values" and hazards in play for modern, long-hitting golfers. The restoration was completed in 1999, the same year the course gained an environmental accreditation from the Audubon Cooperative Sanctuary Program.

ELK WARS

Maintaining a world-class golf course in the middle of an ancient alluvial fan frequented by large, iconic wildlife species is no easy task. While the Banff Springs Golf Course has been visited at one time or another by members of the full suite of predators and prey that grace the Canadian Rockies, none has produced more consistent consternation than *Cervus canadensis*, commonly known as wapiti or, more commonly yet, elk.

Today, elk are a common sight on the golf course.

Although the species had largely disappeared from the Bow Valley when the course opened in 1911, the population rebounded dramatically following an elk reintroduction program initiated a few years later. The elk relished the golf course's open spaces and grasses in summer and winter alike, and it wasn't long before belligerent bulls and defensive cows were presenting golfers with a new understanding of the term *hazard.* At the same time, the course superintendent, Casper McCullough, was discovering the sort of damage sharp hooves and ivory teeth can inflict on finely mown fairways and greens. Elk, he reported, "constituted a worse menace than a player who fails to replace his divots."

Between 1927 and 1986 the golf course was surrounded by a fence, designed to keep wildlife at bay.

From 1927 to 1986, the course was fenced in an effort to keep the elk at bay, but fence breaches, snow drifts, and gates carelessly left open supported the animals' determined efforts to enjoy what one biologist called "a 24/7, 365-day wapiti salad bar." After World War II, Banff school children would be recruited for a spring elk drive, in which they would line up with pots and pans and move through the forest on the edges of the course, pushing the elk toward a gate at the east end of the course.

A more sophisticated ecological understanding and a new environmental ethos led to the removal of the fence in 1986. Today, with Parks Canada pursuing a stringent program of elk control within the Banff townsite, there aren't as many elk on the links as in years past, but they are still around. Their presence and the attendant course depredations, along with the occasional appearance of deer, bears, coyotes, wolves, and cougars, are accepted as an intriguing element of the Banff course, making for good stories at the 19th hole.

The most visual achievement of Kissane's tenure was the addition of an entirely new hotel entrance and lobby. As with other major hotel renovations of the day, the design work was a partnered effort between architect Robert LeBlond and interior designer Kerry Busby. The new space, comprising nearly 2,200 square metres (23,680 square feet)—double the size of the original lobby—was built along the west wall of the hotel, pushing the building's footprint out towards Spray Avenue. Essentially, what was once the exterior western wall of the centre tower became the interior eastern wall of the lobby that greets guests as they enter the hotel.

The lobby foreshadows the grandeur of the hotel's older public areas by featuring a high vaulted ceiling, Rundlestone columns, 20-foot-high windows, medieval chandeliers, hand-carved wooden chairs, and, on the wall at each end of the hall, the hotel's own heraldic badge. Two massive Tyndall Stone stairways sweep up and into the heart of the hotel. The floor, also Tyndall Stone, is covered in sections by handcrafted carpets that echo stained-glass themes and mottoes found in the windows of Mount Stephen Hall. The family motto of one-time CPR chief engineer John Fairbairn is particularly prevalent: *Semper Eadem* ("Always the Same").

On the east side of the hotel, the original lobby has become Rundle Lounge, a gracious, comfortably appointed area with vaulted ceilings, wrought-iron chandeliers, antique furnishings, and seven-metre-high windows that provide panoramic views of the Bow River and Mount Rundle. An adjoining parlour, named for Sir William Wallace—the 13th century Scots knight and leader portrayed by Mel Gibson as Braveheart in the 1995 movie—offers an equally comfortable, quiet retreat with log fireplace and cozy couches. Evoking a strong sense of old-world elegance, the two rooms have become known as the Banff Springs' "living room."

In the late 1990s, a new guest entrance opened on the west side of the main building.

Outside the lower Rundle Lounge, the old covered porch where the doormen once stood at parade rest in their kilts to welcome guests is now used for special occasions, including welcoming dignitaries. Watching over what is now known as the North-West Mounted Police Courtyard is a limited-edition bronze statue of a Mountie armed with a Winchester rifle astride a horse with an RCMP-signatory cropped tail. Purchased from Alberta artist Harry O'Hanlon, the sculpture honours the role played by the North-West Mounted Police in bringing Canadian law to the North-West Territories in the 1870s. Although the Mountie is rumoured to be a likeness of Colonel James Macleod—who famously suppressed the southern Alberta whisky trade

The gracious style of the new lobby mirrors the rest of the hotel.

and negotiated Treaty 7—at least one staff member, with a smile, has remarked that he looks a lot like Ted Kissane.

Much less apparent to the guests than the new lobby and the reconfiguring of the public spaces was Kissane's work on a critical part of the hotel's operational structure. For years, executive chef Martin Luthi—a well-remembered and much-beloved figure at the hotel who oversaw the Banff Springs' kitchens from 1979 until 2013—had laboured heroically to prepare and serve meals for up to 1,600 guests in antiquated, woefully inadequate kitchens designed to serve half that number. One can only imagine his delight when Kissane suggested he completely redesign the hotel's main kitchen (doubling its size) and reengineer the entire food and beverage operation.

While Kissane's physical renovations and additions to the hotel were an important part of his tenure as general manager, equally important was his influence on the hotel culture. While it was true that the staff had taken some strides towards increased professionalism since the 1950s and early 1960s, there was, Kissane knew, much more that had to be done.

Following World War II, the hotel relied to a large degree on summer students for staff—so much so that the CPR used to run special "staff trains" that arrived each spring from the east and returned in the fall. For a variety of reasons—including first-time adolescent freedoms and quantities of smuggled alcohol—the trips are fondly, if foggily, remembered by all who were lucky enough to be a part of them.

The opening of the hotel year-round in 1969 meant more full-time, professional jobs, but service remained uneven and turnover was a chronic concern. That the Banff Springs was part of an internationally renowned resort town only amplified the issue: in the late 1970s, staff throughout the town adopted Trooper's hit "We're Here for a Good Time (Not a Long Time)" as Banff's unofficial anthem. A Canadian Broadcasting Corporation news piece on the situation, filmed in part in Banff Springs' staff accommodation, created a local stir.

Kissane recognized the critical importance of having staff that not only did their jobs well but also believed in the enterprise of the hotel itself. As he told a reporter in 2001, "As much

HERALDIC HONOURS

A building designed as a castle and featuring the crests and mottoes of the families who built the Canadian Pacific Railway should, eventually, be able to sport a heraldic badge of its own.

On June 5, 1998, on the occasion of the 110th anniversary of the opening of the Banff Springs Hotel, the chief herald of Canada, Robert Watt, did "grant and assign" to the hotel "a badge by Lawful authority in permanent commemoration of its long service to the Town of Banff and its historic importance to Canada."

With full heraldic flourish, the badge description (properly known as a "blazon") reads:

Of a mural coronet Or the merlons topped with truncated pyramids Bleu Celeste and encircled with fir trees Vert an antique crown Argent the points charged alternately

with flames proper and water droplets Azure issuant therefrom a beaver sejeant Or wearing a coronet érablé Gules bearing in the dexter paw a torch paly Or and Azure enflamed proper.

The symbolism, as presented in another document with considerably less flourish and Latin, is easier to interpret:

The beaver is taken from the historic emblem of the Canadian Pacific Railway, which built the Banff Springs Hotel in 1888. The torch symbolizes excellence as well as the idea of the hotel being a beacon for travellers. The lower coronet [a simple crown] represents the strong construction of the hotel itself, with the trees indicating its natural setting. The coronet rising from this refers to the Rocky Mountains, with the flames and drops of water alluding to the thermal springs located near the hotel.

The badge was awarded in response to a 1996 petition to the chief herald made by Robert DeMone, then chairman, president, and chief executive officer of the Canadian Pacific Hotels Corporation, and supported by CP Hotels regional vice president and Banff Springs Hotel general manager Ted Kissane. The badge, with its proclamation, is displayed on the wall between the Vermillion Room and the lower Rundle Lounge.

This bronze statue is in the centre of the North-West Mounted Police Courtyard.

The original hotel entrance is now used for welcoming dignitaries.

as anything else, our ability to compete globally depends on the quality of our staff."

To improve the service and secure the loyalty of the staff, Kissane brought a new level of attention to who was being hired and how they were being hired, looking for individuals with both the right skills and the right personality for a given job. Then, with the right people in place, he was ready to share authority, build teams, and institute training programs that imparted a sense of place and an understanding of the hotel's heritage as a Canadian icon. It was no coincidence that the first person he hired at the hotel was a director of training.

"It was a big change," says David Moberg. "After Kissane arrived, we found we were being asked for our opinions, being asked to contribute. We were given a stake in the place. It made a big difference in the way we thought and felt about the hotel and what we were doing there." The strategy worked: during Kissane's tenure, service improved to levels hearkening back to the days of Oscar Wulliman. Staff turnover dropped by two-thirds.

Kissane's belief in the value of heritage, fully evident in his staff training, was also shared with the guests via a special Banff Springs Heritage Program that was created in partnership with a local historian, Bob Sandford, and David Bayne, who was then general manager of the Château Lake Louise. The program included a suite of offerings ranging from hotel tours to interpretive hikes and even a reinstatement of the old Swiss guides' mountaineering tradition, with certified climbers ready to lead guests up the classic Canadian Rockies routes. Also, as part of the construction of the new lobby, Kissane created a special Heritage Hall, where visitors can contemplate vintage photographs and historic hotel artifacts that range from old menus and silver plates to the red plush bench that for decades provided a perch for doormen waiting for guests to arrive.

Kissane also played a key role in managing the hotel's transition into a new era of international corporate operations. In 1999, CP Hotels, after earlier acquiring the Canadian National Railway hotels and then purchasing the Delta and Princess hotel chains, decided the time was right to increase its international profile. Its first move was to add the US-based Fairmont hotels to its portfolio, not only because Fairmont was a prestigious, well-known brand, but also because the name itself was much better suited for an international operation than "Canadian Pacific Hotels and Resorts." Accordingly, shortly after the purchase, CP Hotels rebranded itself as Fairmont Hotels and Resorts.

Integrating the renamed Fairmont Banff Springs with a new international business and new operational systems involved considerably more than changing the letterhead. "The transition could have been a big deal with a lot of drama," one staffer says, but Kissane managed it, as he managed everything else, in stride. "He knew what had to be done and did it, no muss, no fuss. He made it easy for the rest of us."

In 2001, on the 10th anniversary of Kissane's hiring, his hotel facelift was nearly complete. It had taken a decade of hard work and some $200 million, but Kissane had done what he had set out to do by creating a four-star-plus version of Van Horne's vision. No doubt, then, it was with a great sense of satisfaction that he gathered with 500 guests from around the world on December 1 to tip a glass to a new era at the Banff Springs Hotel.

Once bustling with arriving and departing guests, the original lobby is now the Rundle Lounge, a peaceful public space.

The entire hotel is decorated for Christmas holidays, including Mount Stephen Hall (pictured).

Looking upstream to the hotel from the Bow River.

Into the New Millennium

"WE WILL RECOGNIZE THE BEGINNING OF A NEW GOLDEN ERA."

While there was much to celebrate at Kissane's 10th anniversary party, the otherwise buoyant mood was dampened by the events of the previous September. The 9/11 attacks in the United States generated instant chaos for the global tourism industry, and hoteliers everywhere were rightfully apprehensive about the future. Kissane, who had cut the hotel's rates in the immediate aftermath of the attacks for customers stranded by the closure of North American air space, reported in December that the Banff Springs had already experienced 2,500 to 2,700 cancellations. "We are in for a difficult 12 months," he said. But he was also confident the hotel would weather the crisis:

This hotel was built in 1888 and has been through World War I and World War II and the Gulf War . . . I am confident that those who experience the hotel in the new century will discover the luxury and grandeur that Van Horne spoke of so many years ago and we will recognize the beginning of a new golden era.

In fact, the hotel was in for several difficult years. No sooner had 9/11's impact on tourism begun to wane than the first cases of SARS (Severe Acute Respiratory Syndrome) emerged in Toronto. The outbreak knocked another hole in global travel, and Banff's Japanese market, once so lucrative, all but disappeared. As David Bayne said, "It's very difficult to run international resorts without international flights, and the Banff Springs Hotel and Château Lake Louise have been international operations for a long time. Good regional marketing can help, but there is no way it can fill the gap."

Tourism was only beginning to show signs of recovery when Kissane retired in 2005. His replacement was David Roberts, another experienced, visionary hotelier. Born and raised in Kenya and educated in England, Roberts had previously worked for prestigious properties in London, the US Virgin Islands, and Hawaii. Like Kissane and Petrak, he was regional vice president and general manager, indicating he was responsible for not only the Banff Springs Hotel, but also other properties in Lake Louise, Jasper, and Calgary.

The hotel Roberts inherited was a prestigious, beautifully finished property with a storied history, and he was very much aware of the responsibility that came with the job. In 2018, with the hotel turning 130, Roberts said, "The history of the hotel is incredibly important, not just for Banff, but for Canada. The Banff Springs is a treasured Canadian institution, and I look at us—the people entrusted to run the Banff Springs—as the custodians of that institution and its history. We're looking after it for future generations."

As a custodian, Roberts, like his predecessors, has of necessity followed Van Horne's lead.

HERE COME THE BRIDES

As befits a castle of dreams, romance has been a part of the Banff Springs Hotel since the day it opened. It is only natural an architecture hearkening to distant times and places, an alpine setting of the sort that inspired generations of Romantic poets and painters, and long days dedicated exclusively to the pursuit of pleasure can combine to nurture reveries of Camelot.

The hotel has been a popular wedding destination for generations.

It will come as no surprise, then, that weddings are intimately entwined with the hotel's history. About 150—an average of almost three per week—take place at the Banff Springs each year, and it seems that everyone in Canada has had at least one parent, aunt, uncle, or grandparent who was married at the hotel. In some cases, it is a multigenerational affair: one happy couple recently reported that both sets of their parents had been wed at the hotel in earlier decades.

While the hotel offers a wide range of ceremony rooms and settings, the most popular are the outdoor terraces, framed perfectly by the old "million-dollar view," and Mount Stephen Hall, in all its Scots baronial splendour. The Cascade Ballroom is a popular venue for champagne, cutting cakes, and first dances. For more intimate ceremonies, the Angus and Strathcona Rooms, each with a capacity of 20 guests, are favoured choices. The Willow Stream Spa and the golf course are popular amenities for the entire wedding party.

The Banff Springs' role in happily ever after stories extends well beyond weddings. Honeymoons and anniversaries are big business, too. When Scotty Bowman, the winningest coach in National Hockey League history, returned to the hotel to celebrate a wedding anniversary, he confided to resident historian David Moberg that many years before, he had met a beautiful woman in a beautiful place and married her. On their honeymoon, they had travelled across Canada by train and spent a wonderful time at the Banff Springs Hotel. Some four decades later, they were back again to relive those special moments.

"We still haven't figured out how to export the mountains," Roberts says, "and that means we're still importing tourists." With some modern labelling added to an old story, the Banff Springs Hotel of today sells itself as the gateway to the Rockies UNESCO World Heritage Site and all of the experiences visitors can enjoy therein. "Since day one," Roberts says, "the Banff Springs has been connecting souls with the mountains. Today, with the resources available to us and the amenities we can offer, we're in a better position than ever to help make those connections."

The lure of the mountains may be a historical constant, but it is only one factor in the equation of importing tourists. A second factor—a comfortable experience in the mountain environs—was acknowledged with the creation of an amenity-rich palace that allowed CPR guests in the Rockies to "smooth it" when others were roughing it. Today, with a global market advertising hundreds of tempting resort alternatives, a third factor—relevance—comes into play. To be relevant means fully meeting, if not surpassing, the needs, expectations, and desires of an ever-changing clientele. For the Banff Springs of today, revelance has been defined through a focus on exceptional service and exceptional food.

In 2007, the hotel began implementing a Fairmont offering called a "Gold Floor": an "oasis within the hotel" dedicated to the highest possible service standards. With 110 rooms and suites occupying the entire fourth floor of the hotel and a part of the fifth, the Banff Springs' Gold Floor offers

Fairmont Gold Lounge.

STOCK, one of the hotel's 12 restaurants, sells locally-sourced, sustainable food as part of the hotel's innovative culinary renaissance.

the most discerning guests accommodation, amenities, and personal catering that rival any offered by the hotel at any time in its history. Indeed, with its own registration desk, a beautifully appointed private lounge, individualized concierge service, and catered meals (breakfast and afternoon canapés), the Gold Floor is a contemporary echo of an earlier era of elite guests and pampered treatment.

In other parts of the hotel, Kissane's strategy of combining smaller rooms to make larger ones is helping meet the present-day demand for more spacious accommodation. "Even within the constraints of an old building, we have as modern a guest room as anyone could have anywhere," Roberts says. "People think the hotel keeps adding rooms, but it's the opposite. We've actually become a smaller hotel than we were thirty years ago." In 1988, the hotel's room count totalled nearly 850. The number in the summer of 2018 was 757, down nearly 100 rooms in just 30 years.

Aside from the Gold Floor, the major relevance-focused innovation at the hotel has been with the food and beverage service. In 2015, Roberts, working with then executive chef J. W. Foster, launched what Roberts called a "culinary renaissance." With guests increasingly concerned about food security and sustainability, and asking increasingly sophisticated questions about how the hotel procures, prepares, and serves its food, the two men completely rethought what they wanted to accomplish with the food and beverage program. As part of the process, Roberts and Foster systematically assessed the hotel's restaurants, looking at how each aligned with their new thinking. The result was a multiyear program that saw one restaurant per year reworked top to bottom, from menu to décor.

As Chef Foster explained it, "The program has several different pieces. One is a 'farm to table' philosophy, one is a 'nose to tail' approach to the food itself, and one is a 'hug your farmer' attitude." In other words, the food served at the hotel is sourced as locally as is feasible (generally from Alberta and neighbouring provinces) by producers the hotel deals with directly, is grown, raised, or manufactured at as high a standard as possible, is utilized to minimize waste, and supports small heritage farms and local economies wherever practical. Beyond that, the culinary renaissance also means preparing meals that "not only fuel our guests but nourish their spirits." The goal, said Chef Foster, "is to have our meals provide memories that are a major part of the whole mountain experience."

The care and detail afforded the program is remarkable. With few exceptions, the food served at the hotel is variously baked, butchered, pickled, and preserved at the hotel itself, and some of it is even grown in the hotel greenhouse and the microgreen cultivators tended at STOCK Food & Drink.

Beef provides a good example of the way it works. The hotel contracts with a rancher in southern Alberta to raise 40 head of Angus cattle exclusively for the hotel each year. The cows are branded with nitrous oxide rather than a hot brand (which is less painful for the animals), are grass fed, and are individually monitored to track their health and growth. Each animal has its genetic lineage recorded (some of the herd's bulls have the highest fat marbling in Alberta) and receives periodic ultrasound treatments to reveal how its muscle and fat content is developing, which lets the rancher and the hotel know if the cow will provide AA, AAA, or prime Alberta beef. The rancher does his own slaughtering, after which the carcass is transported to the hotel for aging and butchering. As much of the animal as possible is used, and the bones go into the hotel kitchens' enormous stockpots.

In similar fashion, bison, elk, and boar (game has always been popular at the hotel), chicken and pork, and seasonal organic produce come from small, heritage, or Hutterite farms. Chef Foster was proud to note that the hotel has "a great first-name working relationship with the farmers, which allows [the hotel] to call them up on short notice and say 'We'd like some more chickens of a certain size, or we'd like x number of turkeys at a certain weight for Thanksgiving or Christmas.'" His motto, he said, was, "Hug your farmer . . . We rely so much on them. Trying to run a small heritage farm is hard work, and we support them and their communities in any way we can."

The hotel does all its own baking—using a variety of locally sourced flours to produce a wide assortment of breads and pastries—as well as all of its own pickling and preserving for charcuterie items that are specially featured at the 24-seat Grapes restaurant. The main kitchen even has its own specialized chocolate room, in which desserts are prepared and elaborate chocolate sculptures are assembled and carved for special occasions.

An important part of the food strategy is to offer a wide range of choices for guests who are staying several days. To that end, there are 12 different food venues in the hotel, including a smokehouse, a chop (steak) house, a pub, two lounges, speciality restaurants such as Grapes, and a number of international restaurants featuring cuisine from Germany, Italy, Japan, and France. Afternoon tea is served in the Rundle Lounge. Given the quality and diversity of the food, it is little wonder that a young Calgary food entrepreneur designed a special Banff Springs Hotel foodie tour named "Eat the Castle."

Aside from serving the guests, the hotel's food and beverage operation provides a wonderful teaching opportunity for up-and-coming chefs, given its scale and variety. "With all the kitchens and restaurants," said Chef Foster, "and doing so much of our own production, we have a lot to offer." Accordingly, during his tenure at the hotel from 2013 to 2018, Foster increased the number of apprentices at the hotel from five to over 25. While young professionals from across the country apply for positions, some come from the ranks of summer help. Having experienced the hotel and its kitchens, they decide cooking will become their career.

With 12 kitchens, up to 150 chefs (depending on the season), 90 stewards, and 200 service team members and managers, the hotel serves an average of 3,000 meals a day. According to Chef Foster, that comes in at about 1.1 million potential memories a year.

While the hotel has always been closely linked to the town of Banff and its economy, the relationship has occasionally been stormy—as when the hotel insisted on maintaining its platform rights at the train station—and sometimes distant—as during the early years when the hotel considered itself, as one old-timer put it, "head and shoulders above the downtown commoners."

Today, the hotel works diligently to contribute to the community. For example, in 2016 and 2017, it hosted elegant evening galas to raise funds for a Banff YWCA women's emergency shelter. And in the summer of 2017, with the help of hockey greats Glen Sather (who has long-time ties to Banff), Wayne Gretzky, and Mark Messier, the hotel again raised a considerable sum of money for the Banff Community Foundation and the YWCA. In other instances, David Roberts has been very involved with Banff & Lake Louise Tourism, serving as board chair for two terms, and the hotel has promoted its sustainable food philosophy through participation in Banff's weekly farmers market.

Perhaps the most important thing the hotel does for the town, however, is simply make itself available to the hundreds of thousands of visitors who throng to Banff each year. The castle has been a big part of the Banff experience for a long time. As Roberts says, "We keep the drawbridge down and the portals open." As a result, the town's tourists are welcome to explore the Banff Springs and its grounds, and the hotel remains a favourite "must see" destination.

Even as the hotel sends roots down into the local community, it simultaneously works to expand its international reach. The hotel became an internationally owned entity in 2006 when CP agreed to sell its hotels to an ownership group of US and Middle Eastern investors, a move that put the Fairmont resorts in a portfolio alongside the famous Raffles and Swissôtel hotels. The sale did not go unnoticed, with Canadian nationalists bemoaning the loss of a revered Canadian enterprise. One Calgary reporter went so far as to suggest the Banff Springs Hotel is to Canada what Big Ben is to England, implying the sale should be unthinkable. The sale went through, but a Canadian hero emerged in the process when the Ontario Municipal Employees' Retirement System (OMERS) bought into the new arrangement with the purchase of seven of the Canadian Fairmont Hotels, including the three Canadian Rockies resorts.

The sale was, in fact, very much in keeping with the corporate shuffling that is part and parcel of most modern, large-scale international business dealings. Indeed, over the past few decades, the hotel industry has become an intricate cat's cradle of ownership groups, holding companies, brand owners, property owners, and management groups. To illustrate the point, consider that in 2016, the French company Accor purchased the Fairmont-Raffles-Swissôtel portfolio from the previous US and Middle East owners, leaving Accor as the owner of the Fairmont brand, which is held and managed by Fairmont Raffles Resorts International, while OMERS remains the actual owner of the Fairmont properties at Banff, Lake Louise, Jasper, and Whistler.

Fortunately for the guests, all of that complexity remains, as David Moberg puts it, "on the other side of the postcard." For the guests, says David Roberts, the key point is that the hotel remains a Fairmont resort and, beyond that, the Banff Springs Hotel. And for the hotel managers, the key point is that the present owners understand the hotel, know its history and heritage, value it immensely,

Rafting trips along the Bow River start in the shadow of the Banff Springs Hotel.

Horseback riding has always been a popular activity for hotel guests. Here, riders cross the Spray River, immediately below the hotel.

endorse its vision, and continue to invest in its bricks and mortar and programs. "The owners and managers have a very close partnership," Roberts says. "And that's the formula for success."

The 2006 sale resulted in a gap in Roberts's term as general manager. Departing for Singapore and a posting as executive VP for Asia Pacific Fairmont Raffles Hotels International, he left the Banff Springs in the care of Francisco Gomez, who is remembered uniformly as a "class act" who ensured that the quality of the rooms and suites was maintained, expanded an already expansive staff training program, and spent a lot of time conversing with the guests. "It was one of his strong suits," says Marilyn Bell. "He was a very warm, genuine personality, and he loved to get out and talk to the visitors." He also accompanied Marilyn on marketing trips to Asia, where he was well received. "To have a regional VP show up who was also the general manager of *the* Banff Springs Hotel was a very big deal for them. It helped us a lot."

Roberts, who returned to his old position in 2013, emphasizes those international connections. To be successful, he says, the hotel needs a global reach, brand, and marketing strategy. "Given the way the world works today, our success rests in being more than a regional hotel, a national hotel, a North American hotel. Our global affiliations provide a great, reinforcing network that makes it easy for people in every country in the world to learn about Banff and, with equal ease, book a room at the Banff Springs."

As the Banff Springs heads into its 14th decade, with international tourism booming once again, it seems Kissane's prediction about a new golden era was right. The Banff Springs is as successful, as in demand, and as busy as it has ever been.

Today, driving up Spray Avenue, one encounters a small traffic circle where all exits lead to different corners of the Banff Springs Hotel. In the centre of the circle, a statue of William Cornelius Van Horne points to the hotel proper, as if directing attention, if not traffic, to what is perhaps his finest creation. Across the decades, his vision of a castle in the wilderness has captured the imaginations of people from around the world. Through hard times and good, the Banff Springs has become one of those rare institutions that transcends itself and becomes a symbol of a place and time. More than just another hotel or lodging, it remains the home of treasured memories, mountain adventures, close friendships, and the gracious civility of an earlier era.

William Van Horne statue in the centre of the hotel's traffic circle.

Fine handcrafted carpets featuring family crests of CPR notables grace the public spaces of the hotel. Semper Eadem ("Always the Same") is the motto of CPR chief engineer John Fairburn's family.

APPENDIX: PERIODS AND PIECES

The Banff Springs Hotel's décor and furnishings offer exciting opportunities for exploration and enquiry. The information provided below will help interested guests with their investigations.

ARCHITECTURAL PERIODS

Mount Stephen Hall. Mount Stephen Hall is one of the great halls of North America. It is representative of 15th-century Gothic architecture and was named for Lord Mount Stephen, first president of the CPR. Notable features include the floor of Bedford lime flagstones, the stained-glass crests in the windows (see Crests, below), and the great oak ceiling beams that feature crests of the Provinces of Alberta, British Columbia, Manitoba, New Brunswick, Nova Scotia, Ontario, Prince Edward Island, Quebec, and Saskatchewan. Newfoundland and Labrador was not a province at the time the hall was built.

Oak Room. The Oak Room, which adjoins Mount Stephen Hall, also evidences Gothic influence and is noted for its panelled walls and linenfold carvings.

Strathcona and Angus Rooms.
The Strathcona Room and the Angus Room,

private function rooms just off the Alhambra Room, are in the Norman Gothic style. The Strathcona Room has a balcony that opens to Mount Stephen Hall.

Alhambra Room. Originally a formal dining room, the Alhambra Room shows strong Spanish Renaissance influence. Particularly notable are the cast bronze doors that guard the entrance to the room and the plaque of the *Santa Maria* above the fireplace in the foyer. The circular staircase that leads off the foyer offers a good example of the fossiliferous Tyndall Stone. The ceiling to the stairway exhibits some beautiful "mushroom" plasterwork, while the stairway itself is lighted by irreplaceable Tiffany lamps.

Heritage Hall, above the lobby, showcases the hotel's history.

Alhambra Room.

FURNITURE

The furniture in the hotel's public spaces represents many periods and many styles. A partial listing of the pieces includes the following.

Chairs
Gothic chairs, courting chairs, and love seats
Small Princess Mary chairs
Queen Anne wing chairs
Italian folding chairs
English chair-tables
Spanish torchères
Jacobean hall seats

Cupboards and Sideboards
Gothic cupboard
Flemish cupboard
Tudor-style sideboard
Elizabethan-style sideboard

Tables
Elizabethan refectory table
English writing desks
English chair-table

Mount Stephen Hall is a good place to view a variety of period furniture.

CRESTS

Speculation often runs high concerning the crests and mottoes found in Mount Stephen Hall and the Oak Room. Below is a compilation of the mottoes, their translations, and the CPR officials to whom they belonged.

Mount Stephen Hall

Contra Audentior, In Opposition More Daring; George Stephen

Modestia et Fidelitas, Modest and Loyal; Sir Edward Beatty

A Mari Usque Ad Mare, From Sea to Sea; Dominion of Canada

Manu Forti, With a Strong Hand; Lord Thomas Shaughnessy

Nil Desperandum, Never Despairing; Sir William Van Horne

Semper Eadem, Always the Same; John Fairbairn

Solus Christus Mea Rupes, Christ Alone Is My Rock; John Orrock

Omnia Vincit Amor, Love Conquers All Things; Kate Treleaven

A Cuspide Corona, From the Spear a Crown; Michael Delahanty

Oak Room

Callide Et Honeste, With Skill and Honour; William Wainwright

Fidem Servo, I Keep Faith; E. Alexander

Ne Vele Veles, Form No Vile Wish; Charles Ussher

Fortitudine, With Fortitude; A. Allerton

Serviendo Guberno, I Govern by Serving; John Scully

Nec Temere, Nec Timide, Neither Rashly nor Timidly; William Neal

The large windows of Mount Stephen Hall are adorned by stained glass crests.

BIBLIOGRAPHY

BOOKS

Countess of Aberdeen. *Through Canada with a Kodak*. Edinburgh: W. H. White and Co. 1892.

Baedeker, Karl. *The Dominion of Canada: Handbook for Travellers*. New York: Charles Scribner's Sons. 1907.

Bell, Archie. *Sunset Canada*. Boston: Colonial Press, 1918.

Campbell, Robert. *I Would do it Again*. Toronto: Ryerson Press, 1959.

Coombs, David. *Sir Winston Churchill: His Life and His Paintings*. London: Unicorn Publishing Group, 2013.

Dewar, Thomas R. *A Ramble Round the Globe*. London: Chatto and Windus, 1894.

Fear, G. M. *Banff and Its Beauties*. Toronto: MacFarlane. (before 1900.)

Fraser, John Foster. *Canada As It Is*. London: Cassell and Company, 1905.

Gagnon-Pratte, France. *The Fairmont Banff Springs: The Castle in the Rockies*. Quebec QC: Editions Continuite inc.Quebec QC, 2013.

Gibbon, John Murray. *Steel of Empire: The Romantic History of the Canadian Pacific*. Toronto: McClelland & Stewart, 1935.

Gowans, Alan. *Building Canada: An Architectural History of Canadian Life*. Toronto: Oxford University Press, 1966.

Hart, E.J. *Banff: A History of the Park and Town*. Banff, Summerthought, 2015.

Hart, E.J. *Banff Springs Golf Club: Celebrating 100 Years*. Banff: Summerthought, 2011.

Hart, E.J. *Cave and Basin: Banff's Hot Springs and the Birth of Canada's National Parks*. Banff: Summerthought, 2017.

Hart, E.J. *Jimmy Simpson: Legend of the Rockies*. Victoria: Rocky Mountain Books, 2009.

Hart, E.J. *The Selling of Canada: The CPR and the Beginnings of Canadian Tourism*. Banff: Altitude Publishing, 1983.

Ingersoll, Ernest. *The Canadian Guidebook* (Part II). London: William Heinemann, 1892.

Kalman H. D. *The Railway Hotels and the Development of the Chateau Style in Canada*. Victoria: The Maltwood Museum, 1968.

Knowles, Valerie. *From Telegrapher to Titan: The Life of William C. Van Horne*. Toronto: The Dundurn Group, 2004.

Luxton, N. K. *Fifty Switzerlands in One: Banff the Beautiful, Canada's National Park*. Banff, Luxton, 1923.

McEvoy, Bernard. *From the Great Lakes to the Wide West*. Toronto: William Briggs, 1902.

Morton, W. L., ed. *The Shield of Achilles*. Toronto: McClelland and Stewart Limited, 1968. (Particularly, Alan Gowans, "The Canadian National Style.")

Niven, Frederick, and W. J. Phillips. *Colour in the Canadian Rockies*. Toronto: Thomas Nelson and Sons, Ltd., 1937.

Roberts, Morley. *On the Old Trail*. London: Eveleigh Nash and Grayson, Ltd., 1927.

Sladen, Douglas. *On the Cars and Off*. London: Ward, Lock, and Bowden, Ltd., 1895.

Somerset, Susan M. *Impressions of a Tenderfoot*. London: John Murray, 1896.

Vaugh, Walter. *The Life and Work of Sir William Van Horne*. New York: The Century Company, 1920.

Ward, Mrs. Humphrey. *Lady Merton, Colonist*. Toronto: The Musson Book Company, 1910.

Wilcox, Walter. *Camping in the Canadian Rockies*. New York: G. P. Putnam and Sons, 1897.

HISTORIC ARTICLES, PERIODICALS, PAMPHLETS

Alberta Farmer, 1926.

Annual Reports of the Department of the Interior, 1902-1921.

The Architectural Record, June 1889. Great American Architects Series No. 5. A Review of the Works of Bruce Price.

Building, VI. February 26, 1887.

Calgary Herald, Robert Remington, "Banff Springs Hotel facelift unveiled in a difficult time.'"

Calgary News Telegram, 1912-13.

Canadian Pacific Railway. *Banff Springs Hotel: In the Heart of the Canadian Rockies*.

Crag and Canyon, Banff, 1903-2007.

Dominion Illustrated, Vols. I, IV, 1888, 1890.

Edmonton Journal, 1972.

Rogatnik, Abraham. "Canadian Castles: Phenomena of the Railway Hotel," *Architectural Reviezu*, CXLI (May, 1967).

Winnipeg Sun, 1887.

BROCHURE

Key to the Castle
Free brochure available from the hotel concierge.

UNPUBLISHED MATERIALS

Alice Fulmer. *The Old and a Touch of the New*. Whyte Museum of the Canadian Rockies, Banff.

Mrs. W. S. Painter. Tape interview. Whyte Museum of the Canadian Rockies, Banff.

Walter Painter. *Hotel floor plans*. Whyte Museum of the Canadian Rockies, Banff.

Dorothy Whyte. Personal correspondence.

WEBSITES

Canadian Register of Historic Places:
historicplaces.ca

CPR history:
cpconnectingcanada.ca

Canadian Railroad Historical Association:
exporail.org

Fairmont Hotels and Resorts:
fairmont.com

Mountain Galleries, Artist in Residence:
mountaingalleries.com/artist-in-residence

Skyline Hikers of the Canadian Rockies:
skylinehikers.ca

Stanley Thompson Society:
stanleythompsonsociety.com

Town of Banff:
banff.ca

Trail Riders of the Canadian Rockies:
trailridevacations.com

UNESCO World Heritage list:
whc.unesco.org/en/list/304

Whyte Museum of the Canadian Rockies:
whyte.org

INDEX

Accor 145
Adaskin, Murray 87
Admiral's Suite 112
Aemmer, Rudolph 97
afternoon tea 144
Alexander, E. 151
Algonquin, The 46
Alhambra Dining Room 75, 78, 100
Alhambra Room 80, 81, 82, 149
Allerton, A. 151
Angus Room 140, 148
Audubon Cooperative Sanctuary Program 129
Aylmer Park 15
Aylmer, Fred 15

backcountry cabins 90
Baden-Baden 15
Baedeker's Canada 45
Banff & Lake Louise Tourism 144
Banff Avenue 8, 39, 41, 43, 69
Banff Community Foundation 144
Banff Gondola 122
Banff Highland Gathering and Scottish Festival 92-93
Banff Indian Days 42, 43, 91, 92, 93, 94, 97
Banff National Park 10, 14, 46, 117, 121
Banff Norquay Celebrity Ski Invitational 125
Banff Railway Station 2, 32, 49
Banff Springs Golf Course 53, 68, 93, 95, 96, 116, 122, 126, 130
Banff Springs Golf Course Clubhouse 116, 126
Banff Springs Heritage Program 134
Banff Springs Register 48, 64
Banff Springs snail 18
Banff YWCA 144
Banffshire County 15, 56
Barr, Donald 115
Bath (England) 15
Bayne, David 106, 129, 134, 139
Beatty, Sir Edward 73, 74, 75, 77, 81, 151
Beaux-Arts 19
Beil, Charlie 89
Bell, Marilyn 110, 111, 116, 121, 126, 129, 147
Bell-Smith, Frederic Marlett 90, 91
Benny, Jack 96
Bjork, Mrs. Tomiko 119
Bow Falls 17, 30, 31, 34, 40, 57, 69
Bow Lake 39
Bow River 2, 7, 10, 15, 17, 22, 30, 32, 37, 40, 43, 51, 53, 63, 69, 115, 122, 125, 131, 138, 145
Bow Valley 7, 10, 13, 15, 17, 18, 22, 32, 38, 130
Bow Valley Grill 111
Bow Valley Terrace 140
bowling alley 2, 124
Bowman, Scotty 140
Broadhurst, Michael 123
Brewster, Bill and Jim 37, 63, 92, 98
Brewster Company 100, 101
British Columbia 9, 10, 12, 23, 36, 38, 42, 46, 47, 95
Browne, Belmore 90
Buffalo Child Long Lance 72
Burgess Shale 117
Burt, Allan 88
Busby, Kerry 129, 131

Calgary 42, 47, 68, 121, 124, 129, 139
Calgary Automobile Club 68
Calgary Tower 111
Canada Post 108, 109
Canadian National 46, 47
Canadian National Railway 135
Canadian Pacific Air Lines 117
Canadian Pacific Railway (CPR) 7, 9, 11, 13, 14, 15, 18, 20, 21, 29, 38, 42, 45, 46, 47, 48, 49, 55, 56, 57, 59, 63, 65, 66, 71, 72, 73, 74, 80, 82, 88, 90, 92, 93, 95, 96, 103, 106, 115, 131, 132, 133, 141, 148, 151
Canadian Railway Bill 9
Canadian Rockies 11, 13, 14, 38, 56, 63, 90, 95, 105, 106, 119, 121, 130, 145
Canadian Rocky Mountain Parks World Heritage Site 117-118
canoeing 90
Cannon, Joseph 51
Carruthers, Marshall, and Associates 124
Cascade Ballroom 88, 101, 108, 111, 140
Cascade Mountain 7, 14, 15, 52, 74, 96
Castle & Son Manufacturing 82
Cave and Basin 15, 18-19
Cave and Basin National Historic Site 18
Chateau Champlain 46
Chateau Frontenac 20, 46, 111
Chateau Lacombe 111
Chateau Lake Louise 46, 95, 103-104, 106, 110, 134, 139
Chateau Laurier 46
Chateau Ramsey 115
Chateau Whistler 91
Chief Hector Crawler 43
Churchill, William 89
Clark, D. 11
Clark, Joe 118
Cochrane 38
Columbia Icefields 39
Conceit 63, 64
Conference Centre 123-124, 126

Conservatory, the 79
Cooper, Lady Diana 100
Coysh, Reginald 72
CP Hotels 121, 126, 133, 135
CPR (see *Canadian Pacific Railway*)
CPR brochure 29
Crag and Canyon 52, 53, 57
Craigellachie 12
Cree 10
Crerar, Louis 88
Crowe, Randolph 88

Day, David 121
de Baghy, Audrey 117
De Grandmaison, Nicholas 89, 90
Death Hunt 119
Delahanty, Michael 81, 151
DeMone, Robert 121, 133
Devil's Cauldron 95
Deyell, Ron 123
Dickenson, Angie 125
DiMaggio, Joe 105
dining rooms 27, 29
Duke and Duchess of Kent 118
Duke and Duchess of Windsor 97
Duke of Connaught 57, 63

Earnscliffe Cottage 35
Edmonton 47, 111
elk 129, 130
Empress, The 46, 111
Engelhard, Georgia 95

Fairbairn, John 131, 151
Fairmont Banff Springs Celebrity Sports Invitational 125
Fairmont Chateau Laurier 46
Fairmont Empress 46
Fairmont Gold Lounge 141
Fairmont Hotel Vancouver 47
Fairmont Hotels and Resorts 135, 145
Fairmont Le Chateau Frontenac 46
Fairmont Le Chateau Montebello 46
Fairmont Royal York 47
Fear, George 37
Fear, William 41
Field 12, 29, 47
Fields, Gracie 96
fire 71, 72, 73
fishing 90
Fitt, Patrick 123
Fleming, Sandford 14
Fonda, Henry 96
Fort Garry, The 46
49th Parallel 96
fossils 80
Foster, J.W. 142-143, 144
Fraser, John Arthur 90

Gallery Suite 76
Gandhi, Indira 76, 118
Garden Lounge 111
Garden Terrace 140
Gatehouse, the 72, 129
ghosts 108-109
Gibbon, John Murray 88, 92
Glacier House 12, 47
Glacier National Park 47
Glass, Kim 116
Gold Floor 141-142
golf course 52, 53, 90, 93, 94, 116, 122, 129, 130, 140
Gomez, Francisco 147
gondola 119, 122
Gorbachev, Mikhail 118
Gortner, Marjoe 125
Gothic style 18
Grand Trunk Pacific Railway 46, 47
Grapes 143, 144
Gray, Enid 88
Great Depression 86, 100
Gretzky, Wayne 144

Halifax 47
Hamber Provincial Park 117
hand car 7
Harper, Inspector 36, 37
Hart, Ted 10, 68, 69, 90
Heather, Alfred 88
Heritage Hall 134, 149
Highwood River 10
Holliday, George 27
Hong Kong 13
Hoodoos, the 40
Hope, Bob 119
hot springs 10, 15, 18, 27, 40, 127
Hot Springs Reservation 14
Hotel Macdonald 47
Hotel Nova Scotian 47
Hotel Saskatchewan 47
Hotel Vancouver 47
Howard, Leslie 97

Icefields Parkway 39
Indian Grounds 43
Indigenous people 10, 18
Ivor Petrak Room 113

James, Frances 88
Jasper 47, 105, 139, 145
Jasper National Park 117
Jasper Park Lodge 47, 91, 105, 110
Jenner, Bruce 125

Kennedy, Robert F. 125
King George VI 76, 98, 99, 122
King of Siam 100
King, William Lyon Mackenzie 98, 99
Kissane, Ted 126, 127, 128, 129, 131, 132, 133, 134, 135, 139, 142
Kootenay National Park 117
Kristofferson, Kris 125
Ktunaxa 10

Lac des Arcs 14
Lady Merton, Colonist 51
Lake Louise 29, 35, 38, 39, 46, 91, 95, 97, 106, 139, 145
Lake Minnewanka 10
Langemann, Gwynn 10
Leach, Robin 125
LeBlond, Robert 129, 131
Leighton, A.C. 90
Lemmon, Jack 119
lobby 26, 65, 66, 126, 131, 132, 135
Lodge at Kananaskis 110
London Illustrated News 24-25
Lord Mountbatten 76, 118
Lord Strathcona 15
Lougheed, Norman 68

Lougheed, Peter 76
Lower Annex 72, 115
Luthi, Martin 132

Macdonald, John A. 9, 35
Macdonald, Lady Agnes 35
MacGraw, Ali 126
Macleod, Colonel James 131
Mancini, Henry 125
Manitoba 46
Manor Highland Wing 114, 115, 126, 129
Martin, Thomas Mower 90
Marvin, Lee 119
Matheson, Don 53
Mathews, W.L. 31, 43
McAuley, Sam 109
McCabe, Frank 18
McCardell, Thomas 18
McCardell, William 18
McCartney, Colin 123
McCowan, Dan 88
McCullough, Casper 130
McMillan, Thomas 121
Messier, Mark 144
Mexico 117
Minaki 47
Minaki Lodge 47
Mitchum, Robert 105
Moberg, David 118, 134, 140, 145, 151
Monroe, Marilyn 104, 105
Montreal 13, 17, 20, 29, 42, 46, 47, 48, 55, 80, 82
Moore, Roger 125
Mount Assiniboine 38, 95
Mount Assiniboine Provincial Park 117
Mount Cory 10
Mount Hurd 90
Mount Norquay 10, 122
Mount Robson Provincial Park 117
Mount Rundle 17, 59, 76, 95, 122, 131
Mount Stephen Hall 78, 80, 81, 82, 87, 88, 121, 131, 136-137, 140, 148, 149, 150, 151
Mount Stephen House 12, 47
Mount Victoria 95
Mountain Belle 37, 40
mountain climbing 40, 90
Mountain Galleries 90, 91
Mulroney, Brian 118

National Historic Site 46, 121
National Historic Sites and Monuments Board of Canada 121
National Parks Act 14
Neal, William 151
New Highway to the Orient, The 9
New York Zoological Society 92
North Bend 12, 29
North Saskatchewan River 10, 38
North-West Mounted Police 34, 36, 38, 131
Northwest Mounted Police Courtyard 131, 134
North-West Territories 131
Northern Pacific Railroad 14
Notman, William 88
Nova Scotia 47
Num-ti-jah Lodge 39

Oak Room 81, 148, 151
O'Brien, Lucius 90
O'Hanlon, Harry 131
Ohashi, Kai 117
Old Man Goss 7
Olivier, Laurence 97
Olympic Winter Games 115
On the Old Trail: Through British Columbia After Forty Years 67
Ontario 38, 46, 47, 82, 95
Ontario Municipal Employees' Retirement System 144
Orrock, John 73, 151
Ottawa 46, 48
Oval Room 111

Painter Tower 58, 59
Painter, Walter S. 55, 56, 57, 63, 73
Palliser Hotel 47, 55
Parks Canada 10, 111, 115, 125, 130
Pearson, Lester 76
Petrak, Ivor 106, 108, 109, 110, 111, 112, 115, 116, 118, 123, 124, 125, 126, 139
Peyto, Bill 37, 38-39, 40
Peyto Glacier 39
Peyto Lake 39, 117
Phillips, Walter J. 88, 90
Piikani 10
Place Viger Hotel 20, 47
Porter, Cole 96
Post, Emily 17
Presidential Suite 102, 115
Price, Bruce 17, 19, 20, 23, 29, 46, 47, 77, 121
Priestley, Jason 125
Prince of Wales 97
Prince Philip 76, 118
Prince Rainier 76, 118

Quebec 15, 46, 47
Quebec City 20, 29, 46
Queen Elizabeth Hotel 7
Queen of Siam 89
Queen Victoria 35

rafting 145
railway dining stations 12, 47
Reed, Kate 60, 61
Regina 47
Reynolds family 100
Rice Curry 117
River of No Return 104, 105
Riverview Lounge 80, 83, 106
Rob Roy Room 108, 111
Roberts, David 125, 139, 141, 142, 143, 144, 145, 147
Roberts, Morley 7, 67
Roby, Thomas Charles 13
Rocky Mountains Park of Canada 14, 48, 66-67
Rogers, Ginger 96
Rogers Pass 12, 29, 104
Rooney, Mickey 96
Royal Canadian Mint 108
Royal Suite 115
Royal York Hotel 47, 111
Rude Boys 125
Rundle Lounge 59, 60, 80, 82, 112, 119, 131, 133, 135, 144
Rundlestone 59, 61, 115, 124, 131

Rungius, Carl 76, 88, 89, 90, 92
Ryan, Meg 119

Sam's Place 101
Sandford, Bob 134
Sanitarium Hotel 33, 41
Saskatchewan 47, 51
Sather, Glen 144
Schaffer, Mary 92
Schwarzenegger, Arnold 118
Scully, John 151
Shatner, William 125
Shaughnessy, Thomas 151
She Climbs to Conquer 95
Shoshone 10
Shriver, Maria 118
Siding 29 13, 15
Simpson, Jimmy 37, 39, 92
Simpson, Wallace 97
Sir William Wallace Room 131
Skyline Hikers of the Canadian Rockies 92
Sladen, Douglas 33
Smithsonian Institute 92
Snow, John 10
Solace Spa 128
spa 127, 128-129
Spanish Walk 82
Sports Illustrated 115
Spray Avenue 69, 115, 131, 147
Spray River 2, 17, 22, 59, 76, 115, 146
Spray Valley 120
staff accommodation 72, 112, 115, 126
staff reunion 121
Stanley Thompson Wing 129
Stephen, George 13, 15, 35, 148, 151
Stinson, William 113, 126
Stoney 10, 39, 42, 43, 96, 122
Strathcona Room 140, 148, 149
Sturgis, Russell 21
Sulphur Mountain 10, 15, 18, 22, 41, 119, 122, 124, 127
Sunshine Village 125
Surprise Corner 30, 62, 99, 122
swimming pool 57, 74, 87, 113, 127
Swiss mountain guides 12, 37, 134

tally-ho 32, 40, 52
telephones 50, 65
tennis courts 2, 52, 89, 90
Thatcher, Margaret 118
These Mountains are our Sacred Places 10
Thompson, Ross 36, 37, 42
Thompson, Stanley 93, 95, 126, 129
Thomson, William 52
Toronto 18, 47
Toronto Trio 87, 88
Trail Riders of the Canadian Rockies 90, 92
Trans-Canada Highway 10, 104
Trapp Family Lodge 106
Travel Alberta 111
Treleaven, Kate 81, 151
Trudeau, Justin 125
Trudeau, Pierre 76, 110, 118
Tunnel Mountain 6, 17, 122
Tunnel Mountain Campground 64
Tunnel Mountain Course 116
Turkish baths 57
Tweed, Tommy 96
Tyndall Stone 80, 131, 149

Ullman, James Ramsey 97
UNESCO World Heritage Centre 117
UNESCO World Heritage Site 117, 140
University College (Toronto) 18
Upper Annex 72, 115
Upper Hot Springs 15, 18, 41
Ussher, Charles 151

Valley of the Silent Men, The 64
Van Damme, Jean-Claude 125
Van Horne Ballroom 124
Van Horne Mansion 13
Van Horne Pavilion 30
Van Horne Room 113
Van Horne, William Cornelius 11, 12-13, 14, 17, 18, 22, 29, 41, 45, 46, 47, 48, 73, 82, 88, 90, 106, 118, 121, 123, 126, 135, 139, 147, 151
Vancouver 13, 29, 35, 47
Vermilion Lake 10
Vermilion Lakes Road 69
Vermillion Room 108, 109, 111
Vice Regal Suite 76

Wainwright, William 151
Walcott, Dr. Charles 92
Waldhaus Restaurant and Pub 111, 116
Ward, Mrs. Humphry 51
Ward, Sam 58
Waterkeeper Alliance 125
Watson, Cliff 123
Watt, Robert 132
weddings 140
Whiskey Creek 7
Whistler 145
White Tower, The 97
Whitney, Moxie 104
Whyte, Jon 121
Whymper, Edward 40
Whyte, Peter 89
Whyte, William 21-22
Williams, Don 123
Williams, Robin 125
Willow Stream Spa 128-129, 140
Wilson, Tom 17, 37, 38, 41, 43, 93, 95
Windsor Station 17, 20
Winnipeg 23, 46, 52
Winnipeg Sun 21
winter 15, 105-106, 107
Woodworth, Ben and Fred 15
World War II 101, 103, 130, 132
Wulliman, Oscar 100, 134

Yellowstone National Park 14
Yoho National Park 47, 117
Yoho Valley 38, 92
Ysselstyn, Cornelis 88

PHOTO CREDITS

Summerthought Publishing would like to thank the Fairmont Banff Springs for assistance and kind permission to photograph within the hotel. The publisher would also like to thank the following individuals, companies, and archives for permission to reproduce their work.

Andrew Hempstead: frontcover (lower), p. 4-5, p. 46 (lower), p. 59, p. 61, p. 80, p. 107, p. 108, p. 112 (right), p. 114 (top and lower), p. 116, p. 117, p. 121, p. 122 (all), p. 130 (top), p. 131, p. 134 (top and lower), p. 138, p. 142, p. 145, p. 146, p. 147, p. 148, p. 150 (top and lower), p. 151 (top and lower)

Banff Trail Riders: p. 140

Canada Post: p. 109

Cornell University Library: p. 20

Craig Richards: p. 112 (left)

Dave Moberg Collection: p. 21 (photographer unknown), p. 119

Exporail, Canadian Railway Museum (CPR Fonds): p. 17 (ns_25212), p. 26 (a_1956), p. 65 (ns_5936), p. 71 (ns_1533), p. 72 (ns_12727), p. 75 (ns_23847), p. 88 (m_1947), p. 96 (m_231), p. 98 (top; a_7292), p. 101 (m_355), p. 103 (a_6510)

Fairmont Banff Springs: p. 66, p. 76, p. 77, p. 86, p. 89, p. 102, p. 124, p. 125, p. 127 (Rafael de Jesus), p. 128, p. 132, p. 133, p. 135, p. 136-137, p. 141, p. 149 (top and lower)

Glenbow Archives: p. 6 (na-2968-68), p. 16 (na-2977-48), p. 22 (na-2977-1), p. 23 (na-1075-4), p. 24-25 (na-1406-245), p. 27 (pd-233-1-94), p. 28 (na-637-15), p. 31 (na-529-2), p. 34 (na-673-12), p. 41 (na-529-20), p. 44 (na-5035-5), p. 46 (top; na-1804-1), p. 49 (pd-439-2-19), p. 50 (na-2126-19), p. 54 (na-3267-53), p. 68 (na-4465-14), p. 78 (top; na-4465-82), p. 78 (lower; na-4465-52), p. 79 (na-4465-48), p. 81 (na-4465-58), p. 82 (na-4465-81), p. 83 (na-4465-67), p. 84 (na-4465-18), p. 91 (p0005677), p. 92 (na-5566-4), p. 93 (na-633-10), p. 94 (na-4465-19), p. 97 (na-5667-3), p. 113 (na-5654-177)

Ivor Petrak Collection: p. 89, p. 104, p. 110, p. 113, p. 123

Kate Reed collection: p. 61 (top)

Library and Archives Canada: p. 2-3 (pa_012126), p. 35 (pa_025341), p. 48 (a9031992), p. 87 (pa_041133), p. 99 (pa_057239)

Provincial Archives of Alberta: p. 33 (Ernest Brown collection)

Whyte Museum of the Canadian Rockies: p. 1 (v263-na3738), p. 7 (v10-na66-680), p. 8 (na66-617), p. 10 (v527-ng-124), p. 11 (D. Clark), p. 12 (na66-1797), p. 15 (v263-na3530), p. 19 (v527-ps-1-238), p. 30 (na66-543), p. 32 (v92-ng3-1), p. 36 (v484-na66-2018), p. 37 (na66-636), p. 38 (v484-na66-477), p. 39 (top; v85-na66-577), p. 39 (lower; v577-iid-pd-1), p. 40 (v263-na-0936), p. 47 (na33-1885), p. 52 (v263-na-3711), p. 53 (v465-pd1-16), p. 55 (na66-2522), p. 56 (m282-O.S.), p. 58 (na33-32-3), p. 60 (na33-298), p. 62 (v263-na-3725), p. 64 (p9137-347), p. 69 (v263-na-3472), p. 74 (v263-na-3717), p. 95 (v439-pd360-40-004), p. 98 (lower; na66-1488), p. 130 (lower; p110-66)

Every effort has been made to trace the copyright holders and we apologize for any unintentional omissions. We would be happy to insert the appropriate acknowledgements in subsequent editions.

ACKNOWLEDGEMENTS

Forty-five years ago, when I wrote the text for my first book on the hotel, little history had been compiled about Banff or the Banff Springs Hotel. What did exist were several hundred issues of the local paper, the old Park superintendents' reports, alpine journals from both Canada and the United States, several useful books and articles on early Canadian architecture and culture, and a wonderful selection of Victorian travel journals that detailed adventurous trips by rail through the Canadian Rockies. Most of the resources were housed in the Archives of the Canadian Rockies and the Glenbow Historical Archives, whose respective staffs provided much-appreciated help.

The real treasure, however, was a cast of former Banff Springs Hotel employees who worked at the hotel in various capacities throughout the decades. Eager to contribute, they provided me with materials, memories, and sound advice, to say nothing of tea and cookies. Their names constitute a history of Banff and the hotel in and of themselves: Murray Adaskin, Walter Ashdown, Pat Brewster, Dorothy Cranstone, Pat Fitt, Don Harmon, Nick and Willie Morant, Casper McCullough, Sam McAuley, Pearl Moore, Mrs. W. S. Painter, Elizabeth Rummel, Sam Ward, Mrs. Frank Wheatley, Dorothy White, and Catherine Whyte. I remember the hours I spent with them fondly.

A Castle in the Wilderness draws from sources I couldn't have imagined in 1973. Putting aside all the ready resources of the Internet, I am particularly indebted to a number of books and people.

From his perch as director of the Whyte Museum of the Canadian Rockies, E. J. "Ted" Hart spent over 35 years curating, compiling, and writing about the history of the Canadian Rockies and Banff National Park. His many books, on topics such as the CPR's campaign to "sell" the Canadian Rockies and on the Banff Springs' golf course, provided a greatly expanded context, new insights, and some fine stories for my own work.

I also acknowledge France Gagnon-Pratte, whose book *The Fairmont Banff Springs: The Castle in the Rockies* provided details from the Canadian Pacific and Canadian Pacific Hotel Archives that were previously unavailable. Her book contains a wonderful collection of historic and contemporary images of the hotel and a wealth of information regarding its interior through the years.

I am particularly appreciative of the many people who work or have worked at the Fairmont Banff Springs in recent decades. David "Mo" Moberg, David Bayne, and Marilyn Bell, who collectively worked an astonishing 129 years at or for the hotel in a wide variety of roles, were particularly generous with their time. First, they granted me interviews, and second, they reviewed and commented on the last three chapters. Over a period of several months, I came to think of the trio as both my Banff Springs Brain Trust and colour commentators for the decades from the mid-1960s to the present day. David Moberg, who worked at the hotel for 51 years and eventually became its resident historian as well as its manager of guest relations, opened his personal and extensive archives of letters, articles, books, brochures, and photographs—many of his own taking—and has been inspirational in his support of the project.

Of those currently employed by the hotel, and aside from the many staff I engaged in informal conversations, I want to thank David Roberts for giving me insights into the ownership and operations of the contemporary hotel, Chef J. W. Foster for an extended tour of the hotel kitchens and an enthusiastic explanation of the hotel's "culinary renaissance" and apprenticeship program, and Angela Moore and Angela Jacobson for their patience in tracking down answers to my multitudinous questions.

I also want to thank Summerthought's publisher, Andrew Hempstead, for giving me the opportunity to revisit and rework a project I undertook at the beginning of my writing career. Andrew also took many of the photographs appearing in the book. I also appreciate Rachel Small's assistance in editing the text and Linda Petras's design.

Finally, I thank my wife, Barbara Robinson, for her patience, her understanding of English grammar, and her excellent proofreading.

ABOUT THE AUTHOR

Aside from writing *Castle in the Wilderness* and several other books on the human and natural history of the Canadian Rockies, **Bart Robinson** has enjoyed a long career as a journalist, editor, and conservationist. He was an editor with *Equinox* magazine from 1982 to 1994, and the Executive Director of the Yellowstone to Yukon Conservation Initiative from 1996 to 2003. He is now retired and lives in Canmore Alberta. Despite the passage of more than four decades since the first version of his story of the Banff Springs Hotel was published, the hotel remains one of Mr. Robinson's favourite haunts.

Long-term Banff Springs employee and hotel historian David Moberg (left), with the author Bart Robinson on the hotel terrace.